Multicultural Folktales

Multicultural Folktales

Readers Theatre for Elementary Students

Suzanne I. Barchers

2000
Teacher Ideas Press
A Division of
Libraries Unlimited, Inc.
Englewood, Colorado

No part of this publication may be reproduced, stored in a retrieval system, or transmitted, in any form or by any means, electronic, mechanical, photocopying, recording, or otherwise, without the prior permission of the publisher. An exception is made for individual librarians and educators, who may make copies of scripts for classroom use in a single school. Other portions of the book (up to 15 pages) may be copied for in-service programs or other educational programs in a single school or library. Standard citation information should appear on every page.

Teacher Ideas Press
A Division of
Libraries Unlimited, Inc.
P.O. Box 6633
Englewood, CO 80155-6633
1-800-237-6124
www.lu.com/tip

Library of Congress Cataloging-in-Publication Data

Barchers, Suzanne I.
    Multicultural folktales : readers theatre for elementary students / Suzanne I. Barchers
        p. cm.
    Includes bibliographical references.
    ISBN 1-56308-760-X
    1. Folklore and children. 2. Tales--Study and teaching (Elementary) 3. Multicultural education. I. Title.

GR43.C4 B39 2000
808.5'4--dc21   99-052879

Dedicated to the many wonderful Susans in my life:
Susan Carlson, Susan Hill, Susan Ohanian,
and Susan Zernial.

Contents

Acknowledgments

"Arion and His Harp" was adapted from "Arion and His Harp" in *Troubadour's Storybag: Musical Folktales of the World,* retold and edited by Norma J. Livo (Golden, CO: Fulcrum, 1996), 95–97. Used with permission.

"The Bee, the Harp, the Mouse, and the Bum-Clock" was adapted from *Irish Fairy Tales,* edited by Philip Smith (New York: Dover Publications, 1993); taken from *Donegal Fairy Stories,* 1900. Reprinted by Dover Publications.

"Catherine and Her Destiny" was adapted from "Catherine and Her Destiny" in *Wise Women: Folk and Fairy Tales from Around the World,* retold and edited by Suzanne I. Barchers (Englewood, CO: Libraries Unlimited, 1990), 129–32.

"The Clever Daughter" was adapted from "The Peasant's Clever Daughter" in *Wise Women: Folk and Fairy Tales from Around the World,* retold and edited by Suzanne I. Barchers (Englewood, CO: Libraries Unlimited, 1990), 3–5.

"Finding the Foolish" was adapted from "The Foolish Husbands" in *Wise Women: Folk and Fairy Tales from Around the World,* retold and edited by Suzanne I. Barchers (Englewood, CO: Libraries Unlimited, 1990), 265–67. Copyright Storycart Press, 1998. Used with permission.

"Fortunée" was adapted from "Fortunée" in *Wise Women: Folk and Fairy Tales from Around the World,* retold and edited by Suzanne I. Barchers (Englewood, CO: Libraries Unlimited, 1990), 81–84.

"The Forty Thieves" was adapted from "The Forty Thieves" in *Wise Women: Folk and Fairy Tales from Around the World,* retold and edited by Suzanne I. Barchers (Englewood, CO: Libraries Unlimited, 1990), 183–89.

"The Giant in the Garden" was adapted from "The Princess and the Giant" in *Wise Women: Folk and Fairy Tales from Around the World,* retold and edited by Suzanne I. Barchers (Englewood, CO: Libraries Unlimited, 1990), 43–46. Copyright Storycart Press, 1998. Used with permission.

"Gifts of Love" was adapted from "Gifts of Love" in *Wise Women: Folk and Fairy Tales from Around the World,* retold and edited by Suzanne I. Barchers (Englewood, CO: Libraries Unlimited, 1990), 125–26.

"Grateful Hans" by Suzanne I. Barchers (Arvada, CO: Storycart Press, 1998). Used with permission.

"How Fisher Went to the Skyland" was adapted from "How Fisher Went to the Skyland: The Origin of the Big Dipper" in *Keepers of the Earth: Native American Stories and Environmental Activities for Children* by Michael J. Caduto and Joseph Bruchac (Golden, CO: Fulcrum, 1988, 1989, 1997), 117–20. Used with permission.

"The Learned Servant Girl" was adapted from "The Learned Servant Girl" in *Wise Women: Folk and Fairy Tales from Around the World,* retold and edited by Suzanne I. Barchers (Englewood, CO: Libraries Unlimited, 1990), 169–70.

"Legend of the Feathered Serpent" is adapted from "Legend of the Feathered Serpent: An Aztec Legend" in *The Eagle and the Rainbow: Timeless Tales from México* by Antonio Hernández Madrigal, illustrated by Tomie dePaola (Golden, CO: Fulcrum, 1997), 43–53. Used with permision.

"Los Tres Ratoncitos: A Chiste" is adapted from "Los Tres Ratoncitos: A Chiste" in *Una Linda Raza: Cultural and Artistic Traditions of the Hispanic Southwest* (Golden, CO: Fulcrum, 1998), 104. Used with permission.

"The Magic Fan" was adapted from "Patience" in *Wise Women: Folk and Fairy Tales from Around the World,* retold and edited by Suzanne I. Barchers (Englewood, CO: Libraries Unlimited, 1990), 31–34.

"The Magic Table" by Suzanne I. Barchers (Arvada, CO: Storycart Press, 1998). Used with permission.

"The Master-Maid" was adapted from "The Master-Maid" in *Wise Women: Folk and Fairy Tales from Around the World,* retold and edited by Suzanne I. Barchers (Englewood, CO: Libraries Unlimited, 1990), 191–201.

"Molly Whuppie" was adapted from "Molly Whuppie" in *Wise Women: Folk and Fairy Tales from Around the World,* retold and edited by Suzanne I. Barchers (Englewood, CO: Libraries Unlimited, 1990), 87–89.

"Princess Maya" was adapted from "Princess Maya" in *Wise Women: Folk and Fairy Tales from Around the World,* retold and edited by Suzanne I. Barchers (Englewood, CO: Libraries Unlimited, 1990), 231–33.

"Princess Sivatra" was adapted from "Princess Sivatra" in *Wise Women: Folk and Fairy Tales from Around the World,* retold and edited by Suzanne I. Barchers (Englewood, CO: Libraries Unlimited, 1990), 211–14.

"Sally Ann Thunder and Davey Crockett" by Suzanne I. Barchers (Arvada, CO: Storycart Press, 1998). Used with permission.

"The Snow Queen" was adapted from "The Snow Queen" in *Wise Women: Folk and Fairy Tales from Around the World,* retold and edited by Suzanne I. Barchers (Englewood, CO: Libraries Unlimited, 1990), 49–62.

"Spider Flies to the Feast" was adapted from "Spider Flies to the Feast" in *Why Leopard Has Spots: Dan Stories from Liberia* by Won-Ldy Paye and Margaret H. Lippert, illustrated by Ashley Bryan (Golden, CO: Fulcrum, 1998), 23–30. Used with permission.

"To the Sun, Moon, and Wind" was adapted from "The Sprig of Rosemary" in *Wise Women: Folk and Fairy Tales from Around the World,* retold and edited by Suzanne I. Barchers (Englewood, CO: Libraries Unlimited, 1990), 217–19. Copyright Storycart Press, 1998. Used with permission.

"The Tree That Bled Fish" was adapted from "The Tree That Bled Fish" in *From the Mouth of the Monster Eel: Stories from Micronesia* by Bo Flood, illustrated by Margo Vitarelli (Golden, CO: Fulcrum, 1996), 25–31. Used with permission

"Water, Water Will Be Mine" was adapted from "Water, Water Will Be Mine" in *Hyena and the Moon: Stories to Tell from Kenya* by Heather McNeil (Englewood, CO: Libraries Unlimited, 1994), 86–94. Used with permission.

"The White-Haired Old Woman" was adapted from "The White-Haired Old Woman" in *Wise Women: Folk and Fairy Tales from Around the World,* retold and edited by Suzanne I. Barchers (Englewood, CO: Libraries Unlimited, 1990), 319–20.

"The Young Chief Who Played the Flute" was adapted from "The Young Chief Who Played the Flute" in *Troubadour's Storybag: Musical Folktales of the World,* edited and retold by Norma J. Livo (Golden, CO: Fulcrum, 1996), 51–55. Used with permission.

Introduction

The scripts in this collection are drawn from folk and fairy tales from around the world. Although many tales have a universal style, they represent cultural differences that give them a flavor of the country of origin. Many stories will have familiar characters: Dick Whittington, Baba Yaga, the Snow Queen, Gawain, and Anansi. Others might be new: Princess Sivatra, Princess Maya, the Master-Maid, and Catherine. Readers are encouraged to look for parallels to familiar tales and to consider the cultural context of each individual tale while using the scripts.

The Role of Readers Theatre

"Readers theatre is a presentation by two or more participants who read from scripts and interpret a literary work in such a way that the audience imaginatively senses characterization, setting, and action. Voice and body tension rather than movement are involved, thus eliminating the need for the many practice sessions that timing and action techniques require in the presentation of a play" (Laughlin and Latrobe 1990, 3). Generally, there are minimal props and movement on the stage, although with primary students, adding such touches enlivens the production and invites more active participation. The ease of incorporating readers theatre into the language arts program offers teachers an exciting way to enhance the program, especially in classrooms that emphasize a variety of reading and listening experiences.

Traditionally, the primary focus of readers theatre is on an effective reading of the script rather than on a dramatic, memorized presentation. Because many of the scripts are familiar, students will naturally paraphrase their reading, an acceptable practice. Each of the scripts in this collection was evaluated with the Flesch-Kincaid readability scale and grouped into first-, second-, third-, fourth-, or fifth-grade readability levels. Before using, each script should be further evaluated by the teacher for content or vocabulary that might be challenging for students. Because the first-grade scripts have short sentences, students should take care to read them smoothly. Although some scripts have an upper-grade-level designation, they may seem easier than other scripts in the same group because of the story or content. Each script should be considered individually, and students should be encouraged to adapt the scripts to a more comfortable vocabulary whenever appropriate.

The performance of readers theatre scripts encourages strong oral skills for readers and promotes active listening for students in the audience (Sloyer 1982, 4). Students explore literature in a new form, and the class can begin to analyze various treatments of the same or similar stories by comparing these to versions they have heard or read. Students in a ten-week project using readers theatre became adept at going " 'inside' the story, experiencing the thoughts and feelings of the characters" (Martinez, Roser, and Strecker 1998, 332). Students have ample opportunity to reread text, working on fluency and delivery. An additional benefit is the pleasure of performing for parents or other classes and the ease of preparing for special days when a program is expected.

Preparing the Scripts

Once scripts are chosen for reading, make enough copies for each character, plus an extra set or two for your use and a replacement copy. To help beginning or remedial readers keep their place on the page, use highlighter markers to designate a character's name within the copy. For example, someone reading the role of the narrator could be highlighted in blue, with other parts in different colors. This helps readers track their parts and eases management of scripts in the event pages become mixed. Encourage students to find their own techniques for management.

Photocopied scripts will last longer if you use a three-hole punch (or copy them on prepunched paper) and place them in inexpensive folders. The folders can be color coordinated to the internal highlighting for each character's part. The title of the play can be printed on the outside of the folder, and scripts can be stored easily for the next reading. Preparing the scripts and folders is a good task for a volunteer parent or an older student helper. The preparation takes a minimum of initial attention and needs to be repeated only when a folder is lost.

Getting Started

For the first experience with a readers theatre script, choose a script with many characters to involve more students. Gather the students informally, perhaps in a circle on the floor. If a story or picture-book version of the chosen script is available, read it aloud to the students. Next, introduce the script version and explain that readers theatre does not mean memorizing a play and acting it out, but rather reading a script aloud with perhaps a few props and actions. Select volunteers to do the initial reading, allowing them an opportunity to review their parts before reading aloud. Other students could examine other versions, brainstorm prop ideas, or preview other scripts.

Before reading the first script, decide whether to choose parts after the reading or to introduce additional scripts to involve more students. A readers theatre workshop could be held periodically, with each student belonging to a group that prepares a script for presentation. A readers theatre festival could be planned for a special day when several short scripts are presented consecutively, with brief intermissions between each reading. Groups of tales could include princess tales, animal tales, tales from a specific continent or region, or tales of conquest. Consider these groupings drawn from this collection:

Princess tales: "Princess Sivatra," "Princess Maya," and "The Seven Pairs of Slippers"

Giant tales: "Molly Whuppie," "The Giant in the Garden," and "The Seven Pairs of Slippers"

Animal tales: "The Farmer and the Animals," "Los Tres Ratoncitos: A Chiste," "Water, Water Will Be Mine," and "How Fisher Went to the Skyland"

Insect tales: "Spider Flies to the Feast" and "Why Ants Carry Burdens"

Tales of enchantment: "Gawain and the Green Knight," "Catherine and Her Destiny," "To the Sun, Moon, and Wind," "Fortunée," "The Magic Fan," and "The Snow Queen"

Once the students have read the scripts and become familiar with new vocabulary, determine which students will read the various parts. In assigning roles, strive for a balance between males and females. Some roles are animals or characters that could be read by either sex. Some parts are considerably more demanding than others, and students should be encouraged to volunteer for roles that will be comfortable. Once they are familiar with readers theatre, students should be encouraged to stretch and try a reading that is challenging. Though one goal for incorporating readers theatre is to develop and inspire competent readers, it is equally important that the students succeed and enjoy the literature.

Presentation Suggestions

For readers theatre, readers traditionally stand—or sit on stools, chairs, or the floor—in a formal presentation style. The narrator may stand with the script placed on a music stand or lectern slightly off to one side. The readers may hold their scripts in black or colored folders.

The position of the reader indicates the importance of the role. For example, Spider in "Spider Flies to the Feast" would have a position in the front center of the stage, with the minor characters to the sides and slightly behind him. In scripts with many minor characters, the main characters could be on one side of the stage with the other characters entering and remaining on the other side of the stage for their lines.

Because these scripts are appropriate for developing young or remedial readers, it is important that the students are comfortable with the physical arrangement. It is assumed that the students will present informally, perhaps adapting or enlivening the traditional readers theatre style. Therefore, a traditional arrangement for presenters is not provided with the scripts. Instead, a few general suggestions are supplied for each play. For example, readers of brief parts may enter or leave the stage prior to and following their parts. Alternatively, readers may stand up for a reading and sit down for the remainder of the script. This practice is especially helpful for younger readers who may have difficulty standing quietly for long periods.

Determining the presentation arrangement is a good cooperative activity for the readers. The arrangement should foster success; a student who cannot stand quietly for a long time should be allowed to sit on a chair, pillow, or the floor. The restless student with a short reading could remain on stage only for the duration of the reading. However, students may have fresh ideas for a different presentation, and their involvement should be fostered.

Props

Readers theatre traditionally has no, or few, props. However, simple costuming effects, such as a hat, apron, or scarf, plus a few props on stage will lend interest to the presentation. Shirlee Sloyer (1982, 58) suggests that a script can become a property: "a book, a fan, a gun, or any other object mentioned in the story." Suggestions for simple props or costuming are included; however, the students should be encouraged to decide how much or little to add to their production. For some readers, the use of props or actions may be overwhelming, and the emphasis should remain on the reading rather than on an overly complicated presentation.

Delivery Suggestions

In an effort to keep the scripts easy for readers, few delivery suggestions are written within the scripts. Therefore, it is important to discuss with the students what will make the scripts come alive as they read. Primary students naturally incorporate voices into their creative play and should be encouraged to explore how this same practice will enhance their reading. Small groups that are working on individual plays should be invited to brainstorm delivery styles. A variety of warm-ups can help students with expression. For example, have the entire class respond to the following situations that parallel themes in these scripts:

discovering that your best friend has disappeared;

being kidnapped by a giant;

learning you have been tricked;

having to work in a kitchen for a cruel cook;

finding a treasure in a cave;

seeing a bee play a harp;

having someone steal your only source of water; and

having a witch try to roast you.

During first experiences with presenting a script, students are tempted to keep their heads buried in the script, making sure they don't miss a line. Students should learn the material well enough to look up from the script during a presentation; they can learn to use onstage focus—to look at each other during the presentation. This is most logical for characters who are interacting with each other. The use of offstage focus—the presenters look directly into the eyes of the audience—is more logical for the narrator or characters who are uninvolved with onstage characters. An alternative is to have students who do not interact with each other focus on a prearranged offstage location, such as the classroom clock, during delivery.

Simple actions can also be incorporated into readers theatre. Though primary students are generally less inhibited than older students, encourage all students to use action by practicing pantomime in groups. If possible, have a mime come in for a presentation and some introductory instruction. Alternatively, introduce mime by having students try the following familiar actions: combing hair, brushing teeth, turning the pages of a book, eating an ice cream cone, making a phone call, falling asleep. Then select and try general activities drawn from the scripts: rocking, waving, jumping, fiddling, and so forth. These actions need not be elaborate; characters can indicate falling asleep simply by closing their eyes. Although readers theatre uses minimal gestures and actions, they can brighten the presentations for both participants and audience.

Generally the audience should be able to see the readers' facial expressions during the reading. Upon occasion, a script calls for a character to move across the stage, facing the other characters while reading. In this event, the characters should be turned enough that the audience can see the reader's face.

The use of music can enhance the delivery of the play. For "The Bee, the Harp, the Mouse, and the Bum-Clock," harp music may be used effectively during parts of the play. Royal music may be effective during the king's role in "Dick Whittington and His Cat." Signals could be added to foreshadow disaster, such as having a drum boom just before the narrator tells that a piece of ice has pierced Kay's heart in "The Snow Queen." As with props and action, music should be added sparingly, so the emphasis remains on the reading.

The Audience

When students are part of the audience, they should understand their role. Caroline Feller Bauer (1992, 30) recommends that students rehearse applauding and reacting appropriately to the script. Challenge the students to determine whether the audience might provide sound effects during the script, such as joining in with the chant in "Water, Water Will Be Mine." Cue cards that prompt the audience to make noises can be incorporated into the production. Encourage students to find additional ways to involve the audience in the program.

The Next Step

Once students have enjoyed the reading process involved in preparing and presenting readers theatre, the logical next step is to involve them in the writing process by creating their own scripts. Two of these scripts, "Finding the Foolish" and "The Doomed Prince," do not have endings. The audience can vote on how the story might end or the students can script a chosen ending. Consult your librarian for sources of more folk and fairy tales from around the world. The options for scripts are endless, and students will naturally want to translate a favorite story into a script. For an in-depth discussion of this process, consult Part 1 of Shirlee Sloyer's *Readers Theatre: Story Dramatization in the Classroom.*

References

Bauer, Caroline Feller. *Read for the Fun of It: Active Programming with Books for Children.* Illustrated by Lynn Gates Bredeson. Bronx, NY: H. W. Wilson Company, 1992.

Laughlin, Mildred Knight, and Kathy Howard Latrobe. *Readers Theatre for Children: Scripts and Script Development.* Englewood, CO: Teacher Ideas Press, 1990.

Martinez, Miriam, Nancy L. Roser, and Susan Strecker. " 'I Never Thought I Could Be a Star': A Readers Theatre Ticket to Fluency." *The Reading Teacher* 52, no. 4 (December 1998-January 1999): 326–34.

Sloyer, Shirlee. *Readers Theatre: Story Dramatization in the Classroom.* Urbana, IL: National Council of Teachers of English, 1982.

Sources for Additional Information on Readers Theatre: Storycart Press, P.O. Box 740519, Arvada, CO 80006-0519. http://www.storycart.com.

Chapter 1

First-Grade Reading Level

 The Farmer and the Animals

Finland

 Gawain and the Green Knight

England

 It Could Always Be Worse

Yiddish

 Molly Whuppie

Scotland

The Peach Boy

Japan

The Farmer and the Animals

Finland

Summary

When a farmer digs a pit to trap some animals who have been stealing his grain, he falls into the pit and dies. Ermine pulls him out and takes a bite of him. Various other animals join him in turn, take a bite, and help pull the farmer away. Finally, the farmer is gone and the animals turn on themselves. Only the quick-witted fox and wolf stop the bear from eating them, and they agree to be friends.

Presentation Suggestions

The narrator should stand to one side with the other characters lined up in order of their appearances in the story. If preferred, each character could enter the stage when entering the story.

Props

The characters can add props to indicate the animal. For example, the ermine could have a fur collar or stole. The squirrel might have a bushy tale. The hare could have big, floppy ears. The fox could have a red tail. The wolf could have short ears. The bear could wear dark clothing that is stuffed to make him look large.

Delivery Suggestions

Readers can use voices in keeping with the animal. For example, the ermine's voice can be smooth and soft. The squirrel can have a quick, high voice. The bear can have a deep, gruff voice, and so forth.

Characters

Narrator
Ermine
Squirrel
Hare
Fox
Wolf
Bear

From *Multicultural Folktales: Readers Theatre for Elementary Students.* © 2000 Suzanne I. Barchers. Teacher Ideas Press. 1-800-237-6124.

The Farmer and the Animals

Narrator: Once there was a farmer who got tired of the animals stealing his grain. He dug a pit to trap them. But the farmer fell into the pit and died. An ermine found him there.

Ermine: Aha! I have found the farmer! It looks as though he is dead! It serves him right for trying to trap us. I had better take him before someone else gets him.

Narrator: The ermine pulled the farmer out of the pit. He took a bite of the farmer and then began dragging him away. Soon he met Squirrel.

Squirrel: Hello, friend. What do you have there?

Ermine: It's the farmer. He fell into the pit he had dug to catch us. Take a bite of him. Then help me pull him away.

Narrator: The squirrel took a bite of the farmer. Then Squirrel helped Ermine pull the farmer. Soon they met the hare.

Hare: Hello, friends. What do you have there?

Squirrel: It's the farmer. He fell into the pit he had dug to catch us. Take a bite of him. Then help us pull him away.

Narrator: The hare took a bite of the farmer. Then Hare helped his friends pull the farmer. Soon they met the fox.

Fox: Hello, friends. What do you have there?

Hare: It's the farmer. He fell into the pit he had dug to catch us. Take a bite of him. Then help us pull him away.

Narrator: The fox took a bite of the farmer. Then Fox helped his friends pull the farmer. Soon they met the wolf.

Wolf: Hello, friends. What do you have there?

Fox: It's the farmer. He fell into the pit he had dug to catch us. Take a bite of him. Then help us pull him away.

Narrator: The wolf took a bite of the farmer. Then Wolf helped his friends pull the farmer. Soon they met the bear.

Bear: Hello, friends. What do you have there?

Wolf: It's the farmer. He fell into the pit he had dug to catch us. Take a bite of him. Then help us pull him away.

From *Multicultural Folktales: Readers Theatre for Elementary Students.* © 2000 Suzanne I. Barchers. Teacher Ideas Press. 1-800-237-6124.

Narrator: The bear took a bite of the farmer. Then Bear helped his friends pull the farmer. When they felt tired or hungry, they stopped and took a bite. Soon the farmer was all gone.

Wolf: Look, we've eaten up the entire farmer. What are we going to eat now?

Bear: That's easy. We'll eat the smallest of us next!

Narrator: In a flash, Squirrel was up a tree and Ermine had slipped under a bush.

Wolf: The smallest have escaped! Now what?

Bear: Now the smallest is Hare!

Narrator: Hare went hopping across the field as fast as he could.

Bear: Fox, now you're the smallest left.

Fox: I am the smallest. All right, you can eat me. But first, take me to the top of the hill.

Bear: Very well. Let's go.

Narrator: As they climbed the hill, Fox whispered to Wolf.

Fox: Pssst, Wolf. When I am gone, who will be next to be eaten?

Wolf: Shhh. You're right. It will be my turn then.

Narrator: Wolf decided to speak to Bear.

Wolf: Bear, I don't think it would be right to eat Fox. Let's all be friends and live in peace. Let's vote on it right now!

Fox: I agree. I vote to be friends.

Bear: Well, I see no need to vote. You two agree on this. But I must say I am sorry. I am quite hungry!

Narrator: Thus, the three animals agreed to be friends. They lived together in the woods and never tried to eat each other again.

From *Multicultural Folktales: Readers Theatre for Elementary Students.* © 2000 Suzanne I. Barchers. Teacher Ideas Press. 1-800-237-6124.

Gawain and the Green Knight

England

Summary

The Knights of the Round Table are celebrating New Year's Day when the Green Knight arrives. He challenges them to cut off his head with one blow. If he lives, the knight who accepted the challenge will have to receive a blow from him in one year. Gawain accepts the challenge, even though King Arthur insists that it is a trick. The Green Knight's head falls off, but he picks it up and tells Gawain to come to him in one year to receive his blow. On the next New Year's Day, Gawain arrives at the Green Knight's chapel, only to receive a **tap** on the shoulder and the Green Knight's explanation that Gawain has proved his bravery by keeping his word.

Presentation Suggestions

The narrator can be to one side, with King Arthur and the knights next to him. Gawain should be in the center, with the Green Knight on the other side.

Props

The Green Knight can be dressed in green. King Arthur could be dressed in royal clothing and colors. The knights could wear tunics and carry mock swords. The stage could have tables with dishes to indicate a feast.

Delivery Suggestions

The Green Knight should sound challenging, taunting the knights when they are slow to take up his challenge. King Arthur should sound strong. Gawain should sound sincere and determined, especially when he is preparing to leave for the Green Chapel.

Characters

Narrator
Green Knight
King Arthur
First Knight
Second Knight
Gawain

Gawain and the Green Knight

Narrator: King Arthur was having a great feast on New Year's Day. The Knights of the Round Table came to eat and visit. Suddenly a door opened. A strange man entered the hall. His skin was green as grass. His hair and beard were the color of oak leaves. Even his armor was green.

Green Knight: I have come to issue a challenge to the Knights of the Round Table.

King Arthur: What would that be? These are brave and worthy men.

Green Knight: Any one of you can try to cut off my head with a single blow of your sword. If I live, you must come to me in a year. Then I can strike a blow in return!

Narrator: The knights looked at each other. Did this man have magic on his side?

Green Knight: Will no one accept my challenge? Is no one brave enough?

First Knight: We are all brave. But why accept your challenge?

Green Knight: Why is it so hard? I promise I will not fight.

Second Knight: Then where is the sport? It hardly takes bravery to cut off the head of a willing man.

Green Knight: It appears that none of you are brave enough to take the risk!

King Arthur: My men are brave enough. But what is the purpose?

Green Knight: That isn't important. You seem to be cowards!

Gawain: I am not a coward! I accept your challenge!

King Arthur: No, Gawain, don't do this! It's a trap!

Green Knight: Sir Gawain, do you promise that if I live you will take a blow from me in a year?

First and Second Knights: Don't do it!

King Arthur: Gawain, listen to me. Don't let him trap you!

Narrator: But Gawain drew his sword. He didn't want to kill the Green Knight. In fact, Gawain hoped the Green Knight would withdraw his challenge. But the man knelt down, waiting for Gawain to strike. Gawain raised his sword high. He brought it down swiftly. The Green Knight's head fell to the floor. But the Green Knight was not dead! He picked up his head and held it in his arms.

Green Knight: You have given me your promise, Sir Gawain. Meet me in one year at the Green Chapel. I will meet you there and strike my blow.

From *Multicultural Folktales: Readers Theatre for Elementary Students.* © 2000 Suzanne I. Barchers. Teacher Ideas Press. 1-800-237-6124.

Narrator: Still holding his head in his arms, the Green Knight walked out of the hall. The astonished knights watched him leave. Gawain felt the pain of his foolish choice. He knew he would die in a year. The seasons passed and Gawain felt sad, knowing that he would never again see another summer or fall. Finally, winter came and it was time to leave. Gawain went to King Arthur.

Gawain: I have come to bid you farewell. I need to leave now if I am going to be at the Green Chapel in time for New Year's Day.

King Arthur: Don't go. It will mean your death.

Gawain: No, I must go, Sire. My word is important. I will not bring dishonor on this court.

First Knight: Gawain, don't be foolish. You were tricked.

Second Knight: That's right, Gawain. Your promise means nothing to such as he.

Gawain: I gave my word. I will keep it.

Narrator: Gawain left the court on his finest horse. He had to travel many days. Sometimes he slept at an inn. Other times he slept in an open field. The winter grew fierce, and he rode through snow. The land grew wild and he often saw giants, dragons, or goblins. Finally, he came to a cave with walls covered with green moss. He thought this must be the Green Chapel. He got off his horse.

Gawain: Green Knight, Gawain is here.

Green Knight: Welcome, Gawain. You timed your journey well. Today is New Year's Day. Kneel down now and receive my blow.

Narrator: Gawain knelt and bent his head. The Green Knight raised his ax. Gawain couldn't help but flinch at the thought of the ax coming down on his neck.

Green Knight: Gawain, stay still. Did I flinch when you swung your sword?

Gawain: Strike your blow. I will not flinch again.

Narrator: Gawain heard the swish of the ax. But instead of feeling the blow on his neck, he felt a tap on his shoulder.

Green Knight: Rise, Gawain. You have passed the test and will not die.

Narrator: Gawain rose to his feet, dizzy from this turn of events. He was surprised to see that the Green Knight was gone. In his place stood an ordinary man.

Green Knight: Thank you for your faith, Gawain. I have been under a spell placed on me by Morgan le Fay. We wished to see if the Knights of the Round Table were truly brave. You have proved that they are not only brave, but they are also honorable. You may go home now.

Narrator: Gawain got on his horse and rode back to Camelot. He rejoiced that he was still alive and was proud that he had kept his promise.

It Could Always Be Worse

Yiddish

Summary

When a poor man goes to the rabbi for help in dealing with his noisy and crowded household, the rabbi tells him to bring his chickens, goat, and cow into the house. With each addition the house gets even noisier. Finally, the rabbi tells him to take the chickens, goat, and cow back to the farmyard, and the house seems quiet to the poor man.

Presentation Suggestions

The narrator, poor man, and rabbi have the primary roles. The poor man should be in the center with the narrator and rabbi on one side and his family members on the other side. The repetitive text lends itself to reciting almost from memory, and students should be encouraged to learn the script well so that they can look up at the audience.

Props

The characters can be dressed poorly. The stage could be arranged to look like a crowded room, with toy animals placed on the floor.

Delivery Suggestions

The poor man should sound frustrated and bewildered by the rabbi's suggestions. The rabbi should sound wise and calm. The family members should sound impatient.

Characters

Narrator
Poor Man
Rabbi
Wife
Daughter
Son

From *Multicultural Folktales: Readers Theatre for Elementary Students.* © 2000 Suzanne I. Barchers. Teacher Ideas Press. 1-800-237-6124.

It Could Always Be Worse

Narrator: A poor man lived in a small house with his wife, children, and in-laws. It was always noisy, and he never could get any rest. He decided to go to the rabbi for advice.

Poor Man: Rabbi, I need your help. We are so poor that we all live in one room. We get in each other's way all the time. The children constantly talk, cry, and fight. The in-laws are always telling me what to do. My wife and I fight about everything. What can I do?

Rabbi: Promise me that you will do exactly as I tell you.

Poor Man: I am desperate for help! I promise!

Rabbi: Do you have any chickens?

Poor Man: Well, yes, I have a few chickens in the farmyard.

Rabbi: Then just do as I say and bring all the chickens into your house.

Poor Man: But why would I do that?

Rabbi: Just do as I say, and you'll see the wisdom.

Narrator: The poor man went home and brought the chickens into the house.

Wife: Husband, what are you doing? Why did you bring these chickens inside?

Poor Man: The rabbi told me to do it.

Wife: But they only make it noisier in here!

Narrator: The next day, the poor man went back to the rabbi.

Poor Man: Rabbi, I brought the chickens into the house, but now it is even noisier than before.

Rabbi: Do you have a goat?

Poor Man: Yes, Rabbi, I have one out in the farmyard.

Rabbi: Then just do as I say and bring the goat into the house.

Narrator: The poor man went home and brought the goat into the house.

Daughter: Father, what are you doing? Why did you bring the goat inside?

Poor Man: The rabbi told me to do it.

Daughter: But the goat only makes it noisier in here, and it will probably chew up everything!

Narrator: The next day, the poor man went back to the rabbi.

Poor Man: Rabbi, I brought the goat into the house, but it is noisier than before.

Rabbi: Do you have a cow?

Poor Man: Yes, Rabbi.

Rabbi: Then just do as I say and bring the cow into the house.

Narrator: The poor man went home and brought the cow into the house.

Son: Father, what are you doing? Why did you bring the cow inside?

Poor Man: The rabbi told me to do it.

Son: But the cow only makes it noisier in here!

Narrator: The very next day, the poor man went back to the rabbi.

Poor Man: Rabbi, I brought the chickens into the house, but it only got noisier. I brought the goat into the house. It got even noisier. Finally, I brought the cow into the house, and now it is like a barn in my house! What am I going to do?

Rabbi: Go home and take the chickens out of the house.

Narrator: The poor man went home and took the chickens out of the house. The very next day, the poor man went back to see the rabbi.

Poor Man: Rabbi, I took the chickens out of the house, but now the goat is chewing up everything. What shall I do?

Rabbi: Take the goat back to the farmyard.

Narrator: The poor man went home and took the goat to the farmyard. The very next day, he went back to see the rabbi.

Poor Man: Rabbi, I took the goat out to the farmyard, but the cow has turned my house into a stable! It is impossible to eat and breathe in there.

Rabbi: Take the cow back to the barn.

Narrator: The poor man went home and took the cow to the barn. The very next day, he ran back to see the rabbi.

Poor Man: Rabbi, thank you for your help. With all the animals out of the house, it is clean and sweet-smelling again. You've solved all my problems! Thank you!

Narrator: And so the poor man lived with his children, his in-laws, and his wife, happy with the peace and quiet he had found.

From *Multicultural Folktales: Readers Theatre for Elementary Students.* © 2000 Suzanne I. Barchers. Teacher Ideas Press. 1-800-237-6124.

Molly Whuppie

Scotland

Summary

After being abandoned by their poor parents, three children come to a giant's house. The giant's wife takes them in, but the giant tries to kill them. Molly ensures that they escape and tells a king about the giant. The king has Molly retrieve several treasures, outwitting the giant each time. In gratitude, the king allows Molly and her sisters to marry his sons.

Presentation Suggestions

The parents play minor roles and could leave the stage after their readings. The narrator's lines keep the script moving and should be rehearsed carefully. Molly, the giant, the giant's wife, and the king should have prominent positions onstage. If preferred, the characters could be changed to three brothers who outwit the giant and marry the king's daughters.

Props

The children could be dressed poorly. The giant could be dressed in oversized clothes, with stuffing added for size. He could also wear large boots. The giant's wife could wear an apron. The stage could look like a kitchen or a home.

Delivery Suggestions

The parents should sound regretful about abandoning their children. The giant's wife should sound fearful. The giant should sound gruff. Molly should sound brave and then sound taunting when she steals the giant's belongings.

Characters

Narrator
Mother
Father
Giant's Wife
First Child
Second Child
Molly
Giant
King

Molly Whuppie

Narrator: A mother and father were very poor. They had many children. But they could not feed them all.

Mother: Husband, what are we going to do? We have no money. You have no work. The children are starving.

Father: We have no choice. We will have to leave the children in the woods. Perhaps they can find someone who will take them in.

Narrator: The sad parents took their children to the woods.

Mother: Children, go and play now.

Father: We'll come back for you later.

Narrator: But the mother and father never came back. The children walked and walked. Soon it was very dark. They came to a house and knocked on the door.

Giant's Wife: What do you want?

First Child: We are lost.

Second Child: We are hungry, too.

Molly: Can you give us something to eat?

Giant's Wife: You can't stay here. My husband is a giant. He doesn't like children.

First Child: We won't stay long.

Second Child: Please, can't we have some bread?

Molly: And maybe some milk?

Giant's Wife: I'll give you some bread and milk. But then you have to be on your way.

Narrator: As soon as the children began to eat, they heard someone at the door.

Giant: Fee, fi, fo, fum! I smell the blood of an Earthly one. Who is there, wife?

Giant's Wife: It is just three lost children. They needed some food. They'll soon be gone. Leave them alone.

Narrator: The giant came in and ate his supper.

Giant: Wife! Have those children spend the night! They can share the bed with our three daughters!

Narrator: Molly noticed that the giant put straw ropes around her neck and her sisters' necks. The giant put gold chains around his daughters' necks. Molly stayed awake. When everyone else was asleep, she switched the straw ropes for the gold chains. Then she slipped back into bed. When it got dark, the giant got up. He felt the necks of the sleeping children. When he found the straw ropes, he took those children and beat them to death with a club.

Giant: That was a good night's work. In the morning I shall make a feast of those three children.

Narrator: Meanwhile, Molly woke her sisters. They sneaked out of the house. They ran until they saw a palace. Molly asked to tell her story to the king.

King: Molly, you are indeed a clever girl. Do you think you can bring me the magic sword that hangs on the giant's bedpost? If you can, I will allow your oldest sister to marry my oldest son.

Molly: I will do my best.

Narrator: Molly ran back to the giant's house. She sneaked under his bed. After his dinner, he went to sleep. Molly slipped out from under the bed. She reached over the sleeping giant and stole his sword. But he woke up. Molly ran as fast as she could.

Giant: Woe to ye, Molly Whuppie! Never darken my door again!

Molly: Twice more I will come again!

Narrator: Molly ran to the king and gave him the sword.

King: Molly, you have done well. Now your oldest sister can marry my oldest son. But I have another job for you. I would like the giant's magic purse of gold. It is under his pillow. If you can get it, I will marry your second sister to my second son.

Molly: I will do my best.

Narrator: Once again, Molly sneaked into the giant's house. She waited under his bed until he had eaten his supper. Soon he began to snore. Then she slipped out from under the bed. She slid her hand under his pillow and carefully pulled out his purse. But again he woke up. Molly ran as fast as she could.

Giant: Woe to ye, Molly Whuppie! Never darken my door again!

Molly: Once more I'll come again.

Narrator: Molly took the purse to the king. Her second sister was married to his second son.

King: You are quite clever, Molly. Now if only you could bring me the giant's ring of invisibility that he wears on his finger, I will marry you to my youngest son.

Molly: I will do my best, sir.

Narrator: One last time, Molly hid under the giant's bed. Soon he began to snore. She reached for his hand. She pulled and pulled until she got the ring off. Then the giant woke and caught her by the hand.

Giant: Now I have you, Molly Whuppie. You think you are so clever! Now tell me this. If I had served you as you've served me, what would you do with me?

Molly: Sir, I would put you into a sack with the cat and dog. I would hang the sack on the wall. Then I would go into the woods and find the biggest stick. I'd use that stick to beat the sack till you were dead.

Giant: So be it, Molly Whuppie. That is exactly what I am going to do!

Narrator: The giant put Molly, the cat, and the dog into a sack. He hung it up on the wall and went into the wood to hunt for a stick. Molly began to chant.

Molly: If you could see what I see! If you could see what I see!

Giant's Wife: What do you see, Molly?

Molly: If you could see what I see! If you could see what I see!

Giant's Wife: Molly, what do you see?

Narrator: But Molly wouldn't answer.

Giant's Wife: Well, I will just have to come in and see for myself.

Narrator: The giant's wife let Molly out so she could climb in.

Giant's Wife: I don't see a thing, Molly. Let me out now.

Narrator: But Molly hid behind the door. Soon the giant returned with a huge stick in his hand. He took down the sack and began to beat it.

Giant's Wife: Stop that! It's me, your wife!

Narrator: But the dog barked and the cat screeched. The giant couldn't tell she was indeed his wife. Molly felt sorry for the wife and came out from behind the door. The giant saw her and began to run after her. They ran and ran until Molly crossed over the bridge.

Giant: Woe to ye, Molly Whuppie! Never ye come again!

Molly: Never more will I come!

Narrator: Molly took the ring to the king. She married the king's youngest son and never saw the giant again.

The Peach Boy

Japan

Summary

An old man and woman live simply. But they wished for a son. When the old woman finds a huge peach in the river, she and her husband are delighted to discover a baby boy inside. They raise him as their son, but when he turns fifteen years old he leaves home to defeat the evil ogres. With the help of some animals, he succeeds and brings back enough riches to support his family.

Presentation Suggestions

The narrator should stand to one side with the other characters across the stage in the order of their presentations. Momotaro should stand forward because his role is central to the story.

Props

If possible, obtain some Japanese vases, paintings, or artifacts. The characters could wear kimonos if they are available. A bowl of peaches could decorate a table. A mural of a rugged seacoast with cherry tree could serve as a backdrop. Consider playing some Japanese flute music as an introduction.

Delivery Suggestions

The ogre should use a gruff voice at first, and then he should have a pleading voice. The other characters can use normal voices. If desired, add more ogres to the script, having them speak in unison.

Characters

Narrator
Old Woman
Old Man
Momotaro
Dog
Monkey
Bird
Ogre

The Peach Boy

Narrator: Long ago, there was a little village in Japan. An old woodcutter lived there with his wife. They were poor, but happy. They had a small home and enough to eat. But they were sad about one thing: They had never had a child, and now they were too old. One day the man went out to cut some wood. The old woman went to the river to wash some clothes. She saw something floating down the river.

Old Woman: Look at that peach! I've never seen anything so big!

Narrator: The old woman pulled the peach out of the river. It was very soft and smelled good.

Old Woman: What a fine peach! Wait till my husband sees it!

Narrator: Later, the old woman took the clothes and peach home. Soon her husband came home.

Old Woman: I have a surprise for you, dear husband.

Old Man: What would that be, my wife?

Old Woman: I was washing clothes, and something floated down the river. It came right to me.

Old Man: There are lots of things in the river, dear.

Old Woman: But not like this. Look at this peach!

Old Man: You are right! That's an amazing peach! And you didn't have to pay for it! It will taste very sweet!

Narrator: The old man took out his knife to cut open the peach. Just then the peach fell apart. In the middle sat a little baby boy! He held out his arms to the old man and woman.

Old Woman: A baby! Look at this! We have a son!

Old Man: This is surely a gift from the gods!

Narrator: The old man and woman named the baby Momotaro, or Little Peach Boy. They brought the Little Peach Boy up as their son, happy with their luck. The years passed quickly. When Momotaro was fifteen years old, he talked to his parents about their future.

Momotaro: Mother and Father, you have been good parents to me. Now I must prepare to take care of you. I will be gone for a while. But when I come back, you'll never have to worry about money again.

From *Multicultural Folktales: Readers Theatre for Elementary Students.* © 2000 Suzanne I. Barchers. Teacher Ideas Press. 1-800-237-6124.

Old Woman: But where are you going?

Momotaro: I am going to an island in the far north. Some rich ogres live there. They often rob and kill people. I am going to crush them. Then I will bring back some of their riches.

Old Man: I know about those ogres. They eat humans! How could a young boy beat them?

Momotaro: Remember, Father. I am the Little Peach Boy. I can do things no other boy can do!

Narrator: Momotaro set out. Soon he met a thin dog.

Dog: Do you have something to eat? I'm hungry!

Momotaro: Of course! Here's a rice ball.

Narrator: The dog followed him. Soon a monkey came down from a tree.

Monkey: Do you have something to eat? I'm hungry!

Momotaro: Of course! Here's a rice ball.

Narrator: The monkey joined the dog as Momotaro walked on. Soon a bird flew down.

Bird: Do you have something to eat? I'm hungry!

Momotaro: Of course! Here's a rice ball.

Narrator: Momotaro and his friends kept walking. Soon they came to the sea.

Dog: What is that?

Monkey: I've heard about this water.

Bird: And I've seen it! It's the sea.

Momotaro: We have to get across it to the island. Let's gather up the driftwood. We'll make a raft.

Narrator: Soon they were on their raft floating on the water. A thick fog covered the water. But in a while Momotaro saw the island. They got to the shore and started toward the castle. They came to a high wall and a locked gate.

Momotaro: Bird, fly over the wall. See if there are any ogres around.

Bird: The ogres are all inside the castle.

Momotaro: Monkey, climb over the wall and unlock the gate.

Narrator: The monkey opened the gate. Momotaro and the dog went inside. They made their plan. Then Momotaro began to yell.

Momotaro: Ogres! Momotaro is here! I have come to crush you! Come out!

Narrator: The ogres came rushing out of the castle. They were ugly and carried big clubs. Their leader looked at Momotaro with scorn.

Ogre: You are a fool! We are going to eat you and your friends!

Narrator: But the animals began their attack. The bird pecked at the ogres' eyes. The dog bit their toes and legs. The monkey swung from one to another, biting and scratching them. The ogres begged the animals to stop. Momotaro held the leader of the ogres. He tried to get free, but Momotaro was too strong for him.

Momotaro: Do you give up?

Ogre: Yes! Yes! Make them stop!

Momotaro: First, you have to agree to something.

Ogre: Anything! What do you want?

Momotaro: Pull out your horns. Now!

Narrator: The ogres began pulling out their horns. Without their horns they became quite tame. But Momotaro still had to punish them.

Momotaro: Bring out your treasure.

Narrator: The ogres brought out their gold, jewels, and silks. They took them to Momotaro. He chose what he wanted and loaded them into a cart. Then he and the animals set out for home. And so Momotaro brought riches back to his parents. They never had to worry for the rest of their long, happy lives.

Chapter 2

Second-Grade Reading Level

Baba Yaga

Russia

Summary

When the cat and sparrow leave home, they tell the brave lad to not say a word to Baba Yaga should she come by to count the spoons. But when Baba Yaga comes, the brave lad can't resist telling her to leave his spoon alone. She captures the lad, and the cat and sparrow have to rescue him. The third time Baba Yaga appears, she carries the lad to her home, where she tells each of her three daughters in turn to roast him for dinner. Each time, he tricks the daughters into the pan, roasting them instead. Finally, he tricks Baba Yaga and roasts her as well. Students can compare this story to other Baba Yaga tales.

Presentation Suggestions

The narrator should stand to one side, with the cat and sparrow next. The brave lad should be in the center, with Baba Yaga and her daughters on his other side.

Props

The stage could look like a simple home, with a table with spoons on it. The brave lad should be dressed simply. Baba Yaga could wear a triangle-shaped scarf.

Delivery Suggestions

Baba Yaga should sound evil. The daughters should sound gullible. The brave lad should sound ingenious when tricking the daughters and Baba Yaga into getting into the roasting pan.

Characters

Narrator
Cat
Sparrow
Brave Lad
Baba Yaga
First Daughter
Second Daughter

From *Multicultural Folktales: Readers Theatre for Elementary Students.* © 2000 Suzanne I. Barchers. Teacher Ideas Press. 1-800-237-6124.

Baba Yaga

Narrator: Once upon a time there lived in a cottage a cat, a sparrow, and a brave lad. The cat and the sparrow went to the forest to chop wood. Before they left, they spoke to the lad.

Cat: Keep the house while we are gone.

Sparrow: But if Baba Yaga comes to count the spoons, don't say a word.

Brave Lad: Very well. I'll just sit by the stove while you're gone.

Narrator: The cat and the sparrow went away. Suddenly, Baba Yaga came in. She began counting the spoons.

Baba Yaga: This is the cat's spoon. This is the sparrow's spoon. This is the brave lad's spoon.

Narrator: The brave lad couldn't stop himself from speaking out.

Brave Lad: Don't touch my spoon!

Narrator: Baba Yaga grabbed the lad and flew off with him. The brave lad cried out for help.

Brave Lad: Cat, run! Sparrow, fly! Help me!

Narrator: They heard him and rushed to help. The cat scratched Baba Yaga, and the sparrow pecked at her. The brave lad escaped and they returned home. The next day, the cat and sparrow again prepared to go out and chop wood.

Cat: We are going to go chop wood. If Baba Yaga comes again, don't say anything.

Sparrow: We'll be a long way away this time.

Narrator: As soon as the brave lad sat down by the stove, Baba Yaga came in. Once again, she began counting the spoons.

Baba Yaga: This is the cat's spoon. This is the sparrow's spoon. This is the brave lad's spoon.

Narrator: Once again, the brave lad couldn't stop himself from speaking out.

Brave Lad: Don't touch my spoon!

Narrator: Just as before, Baba Yaga grabbed the lad and flew off with him. The brave lad cried out for help.

Brave Lad: Cat, run! Sparrow, fly! Help me!

Narrator: They heard him and rushed to help. The cat scratched Baba Yaga, and the sparrow pecked at her. Once again the brave lad escaped, and they all returned home. The next day, the cat and sparrow again prepared to go out and chop wood.

Cat: We are leaving now to chop wood.

Sparrow: If Baba Yaga comes to count the spoons, be sure to be quiet. We'll be even farther away today.

Narrator: As soon as the brave lad sat down by the stove, Baba Yaga came in. Once again, she began counting the spoons.

Baba Yaga: This is the cat's spoon. This is the sparrow's spoon. This is the brave lad's spoon.

Narrator: Once again, the brave lad couldn't stop himself from speaking out.

Brave Lad: Don't touch my spoon!

Narrator: Just as before, Baba Yaga grabbed the lad and flew off with him. The brave lad cried out for help.

Brave Lad: Cat, run! Sparrow, fly! Help me!

Narrator: But this time they were too far away to hear. Baba Yaga took him home and put him in a shed by the stove. She spoke to one of her daughters.

Baba Yaga: Daughter, I am going to Russia. Roast this brave lad so that he is ready for my dinner.

First Daughter: Very well, mother.

Narrator: The daughter started the fire. Finally, the stove was hot. She told the brave lad to come out of the shed.

First Daughter: Lie down on the roasting pan.

Narrator: The brave lad lay down and held one foot high. He put the other foot on the floor.

First Daughter: Not like that!

Brave Lad: How then? Show me!

First Daughter: Like this!

Narrator: Baba Yaga's daughter lay down on the roasting pan. The brave lad pushed the pan into the oven. He went back into the shed to wait for Baba Yaga. Soon she returned.

Baba Yaga: Now I am going to feast on the brave lad's meat and bones.

Brave Lad: Feast on your daughter's bones!

Narrator: Baba Yaga jumped! She looked in the oven. She saw that her daughter was all roasted.

Baba Yaga: You won't get away from me!

Narrator: Baba Yaga called her second daughter.

Baba Yaga: Roast the brave lad. I'll be back later and I want to have him for my dinner.

Second Daughter: Yes, mother.

Narrator: Baba Yaga's second daughter made a fire in the stove.

Second Daughter: Lie down in that roasting pan.

Narrator: The brave lad lay down and held one foot high. He put the other foot on the floor.

Second Daughter: Not like that!

Brave Lad: How then? Show me!

Second Daughter: Like this!

Narrator: Baba Yaga's daughter lay down on the roasting pan. The brave lad pushed the pan into the oven. He went back into the shed to wait for Baba Yaga. Soon she returned.

Baba Yaga: Now I am going to feast on the brave lad's meat and bones.

Brave Lad: Feast on your daughter's bones!

Narrator: Once again, Baba Yaga looked into the stove and found her daughter roasted.

Baba Yaga: Just wait, you scoundrel! You won't get away!

Narrator: Baba Yaga ordered her youngest daughter to roast the brave lad. But he shoved her into the oven, too. Baba Yaga flew into a rage when she found out what he had done.

Baba Yaga: This time you won't get away! I'll roast you myself! Get out here and lie in this pan!

Narrator: Once again, the brave lad lay down and held one foot high. He put the other foot on the floor.

Baba Yaga: Not that way! Not that way!

Brave Lad: How then? Show me!

Narrator: Baba Yaga curled up in the pan. The brave lad quickly shoved her into the stove. Then he ran home and told the cat and sparrow what he had done.

Brave Lad: And you never have to worry about Baba Yaga counting our spoons again!

The Bee, the Harp, the Mouse, and the Bum-Clock

Ireland

Summary

In this variant of "Jack and the Beanstalk," Jack trades three cows for some entertaining creatures. Although they entertain his mother, she despairs of having any meat or money. Jack learns that the king is offering a reward of marriage and his kingdom to anyone who can make his daughter laugh. Jack succeeds and marries the daughter.

Presentation Suggestions

The narrator, mother, and Jack have the primary roles and should be positioned prominently onstage. The women and guard could sit until they read their lines.

Props

Jack and his mother should be dressed poorly. The man and woman can be dressed in simple clothing. The guard could be dressed in any sort of uniform or simply carry a mock sword. A mural could portray a castle in the background. The stage could be decorated with hay, a cowbell, or farming implements.

Delivery Suggestions

Jack should sound gullible and eager to please. His mother should sound frustrated with Jack's inability to sell the cows. The man should sound smooth and somewhat sneaky.

Characters

Narrator
Mother
Jack
Man
Woman
Guard

From *Multicultural Folktales: Readers Theatre for Elementary Students.* © 2000 Suzanne I. Barchers. Teacher Ideas Press. 1-800-237-6124.

The Bee, the Harp, the Mouse, and the Bum-Clock

Narrator: Once there was a widow. She had one son, called Jack. They owned just three cows. They lived well for a long time. But at last hard times came to them. Even their crops failed. The poor widow decided she had to sell one of the cows.

Mother: Jack, go to the fair to sell the brown cow. We need the money.

Jack: All right, Mother.

Narrator: The next morning, Jack got up early. He took the cow to the fair. When he got there he saw a crowd in the street. He went to see what the crowd was looking at. There was a man with a mouse, a bum-clock, which is a cockroach, and a bee with a wee harp. The man whistled and the bee began to play the harp. The mouse and the bum-clock began to waltz with each other. All the people began to dance, too. When the animals were done, the man picked them up. He began to talk to Jack.

Man: Jack, how would you like to be master of one of these animals?

Jack: I would like it fine!

Man: Then let's make a trade.

Jack: But I have no money.

Man: Oh, you have a fine cow. I will give you the bee and the harp for your cow.

Jack: But my mother is sad at home. I have to sell this cow to make her feel better.

Man: But when your mother sees the bee play the harp, she will laugh and laugh.

Jack: That will be grand!

Narrator: Jack made the trade. He went home to his mother.

Mother: I see you have sold the cow.

Jack: I have.

Mother: Did you do well?

Jack: I did very well!

Mother: How much did you get for her?

Jack: I got something better than money for her.

Mother: Oh, Jack! What have you done?

Jack: Just look at this, Mother!

From *Multicultural Folktales: Readers Theatre for Elementary Students.* © 2000 Suzanne I. Barchers. Teacher Ideas Press. 1-800-237-6124.

Narrator: Jack took the bee and harp out of his pocket. The bee began to play. His mother laughed and laughed. They began to dance. But when the bee stopped playing, Jack's mother started thinking.

Jack: You have been foolish. We have no food or money. And now one of our cows is gone. Tomorrow take the black cow to the fair and sell her.

Narrator: The next morning, Jack led the black cow to the fair. Once again, there was a big crowd in the street. Jack soon saw the man with the mouse and the bum-clock. The animals began to dance. Everyone danced and jigged along. When they were done, the man saw Jack.

Man: Jack, how would you like to have this mouse?

Jack: I'd like that very much. But I cannot.

Man: Why not?

Jack: I have no money. My mother sent me to the fair to sell this cow. She needs the money to lift her heart.

Man: But if she saw the mouse dancing to the bee's playing, she would surely laugh with joy.

Jack: But I have no money.

Man: Well, I'll take your cow in trade.

Narrator: Jack thought that would be a grand trade. Soon he was home with the mouse.

Mother: Jack, I see you have sold the cow.

Jack: Yes, Mother.

Mother: Did you sell her well?

Jack: I did very well!

Mother: How much money did you get for her?

Jack: I didn't get any money. I got something better.

Mother: Oh, Jack. What do you mean?

Jack: Just watch, Mother.

Narrator: Jack set the mouse on the floor. Then he whistled for the bee to start playing the harp. The mouse began to dance. Soon his mother was laughing and dancing. But when they were done, she got angry with Jack.

From *Multicultural Folktales: Readers Theatre for Elementary Students.* © 2000 Suzanne I. Barchers. Teacher Ideas Press. 1-800-237-6124.

Mother: Jack, you have been very foolish. We have no money or meat. And now we have only one cow left. Tomorrow you must take it to the fair and sell her. Get something to lift my heart.

Narrator: The next morning, Jack took the last cow to the fair. He saw a crowd gathered in the street. The same man had the bum-clock dancing and jigging. Everyone joined in the fun. When they were done, the man saw Jack.

Man: Jack, you really must have this bum-clock. It goes with the others.

Jack: But I have no money.

Man: But you have a cow. We could trade!

Jack: But my mother is very sad. She sent me to sell the cow and lift her heart.

Man: But the bum-clock will lift her heart. Just think how she'll laugh when she sees it dancing with the other animals.

Jack: That is true. I think I will trade with you.

Narrator: Soon Jack was home with the bum-clock.

Mother: Jack, I see you have sold the cow.

Jack: Yes, Mother.

Mother: Did you sell her well?

Jack: I did very well!

Mother: How much money did you get for her?

Jack: I didn't get any money. I got something better.

Mother: Oh, no, Jack. What now?

Jack: Just watch, Mother.

Narrator: Jack set the bum-clock on the floor. Then he whistled for the bee to start playing the harp. The bum-clock and the mouse danced together. His mother laughed and danced. But when they were done, she got angry with Jack. She scolded him and then began to cry.

Jack: I have been a fool. What shall I do now?

Narrator: Jack went for a walk to think about his problem. He met a woman along the way.

Woman: Hello, Jack.

From *Multicultural Folktales: Readers Theatre for Elementary Students.* © 2000 Suzanne I. Barchers. Teacher Ideas Press. 1-800-237-6124.

Jack: Good morning, ma'am.

Woman: Are you on your way to see the king's daughter?

Jack: What do you mean?

Woman: Haven't you heard? She hasn't laughed for seven years. The king will give her in marriage to the man who makes her laugh. He'll also give his kingdom.

Jack: If that is true, I must be off.

Narrator: Jack went back to the house. He gathered up the bee, the harp, the mouse, and the bum-clock. Then his told his mother good-bye and hurried off. Soon he reached the castle. He saw a ring of spikes all around the castle. A head was on each spike. He spoke to a guard.

Jack: Whose heads are these?

Guard: These are men who tried to make the king's daughter laugh. The king has ordered death for anyone who fails to make her laugh three times.

Jack: Can you tell the king that I want to try?

Guard: You're sure? Look all around you, son.

Jack: Just send the message, please.

Narrator: Soon the court gathered together to watch Jack. He took out the bee, the harp, the mouse, and the bum-clock. He tied a string to each of them and led them into the court. When he entered the court, he looked foolish in his raggedy clothes, leading his animals. The king and queen began to laugh. Their daughter looked up to see what was funny. She began to laugh for the first time in seven years.

Jack: Thank you, my lady. I have won the first of the three parts. Just watch.

Narrator: Jack drew his animals into a circle. He began to whistle. The bee played the harp. The mouse and the bum-clock danced together. Everyone in the castle danced along. The king's daughter opened her mouth and laughed a second time.

Jack: Thank you, my lady. I have won the second of the three parts. Just watch.

Narrator: The animals kept playing and dancing. But the king's daughter did not laugh again. Finally, the mouse turned on its heel. It's tail went into the bum-clock's mouth. The bum-clock began to cough and cough. The king's daughter saw this and began to laugh louder than before.

From *Multicultural Folktales: Readers Theatre for Elementary Students.* © 2000 Suzanne I. Barchers. Teacher Ideas Press. 1-800-237-6124.

Jack: Thank you, my lady. Now I have won all of you.

Narrator: The king took Jack and his animals away to prepare them for the wedding. Jack was washed and combed and dressed in a suit of silk and satin. The king's daughter said that he was as fine a fellow as she had ever seen. Jack sent for his mother, who came for the wedding. The wedding lasted nine days and nine nights. Each night was better than the one before. Everyone celebrated, including the bee, the harp, the mouse, and the bum-clock. And Jack's mother's heart was lifted!

The Giant in the Garden

Scotland

Summary

Due to misfortune, a queen has to live on a farm with her three children. When a giant steals cabbages from the garden, each child tries to stop the giant. When the giant kidnaps each in turn, the youngest child tricks him into returning the children to their mother.

Presentation Suggestions

With the exception of the traveler, all characters should stay onstage throughout the play. Although the script calls for two sisters and a brother, the script could be altered to change the roles to any mix of boys or girls.

Props

The giant could be dressed in clothes that are stuffed with pillows, wear oversized boots, and stand on a stool. Garden implements could decorate the stage.

Delivery Suggestions

The reading of the parts should be expressive, with the children showing their outrage at the giant's thefts and kidnappings. The queen should sound controlled and calm. The giant should use a big, gruff voice.

Characters

Narrator
Queen
Oldest Child
Middle Child
Youngest Child
Giant
Traveler

The Giant in the Garden

Narrator: Once upon a time in a faraway land, a king died. The queen and her three children had to live on a small farm. The queen had always worked hard, so she decided to make the best of her new life. She talked to her children about their new way of life.

Queen: Children, we have a lot of work to do. We need to tend the garden first. Then we will have food to eat.

Oldest Child: I wish we didn't have to work so hard.

Queen: I know, dear. But we can make the best of it.

Narrator: One morning, the middle child went to the garden. She wanted to get a cabbage for the family's dinner. She rushed back into the house.

Middle Child: Mother! Look! Someone has taken a whole row of cabbages from our garden!

Narrator: They all rushed out to the garden.

Youngest Child: Oh, no! Look at the mess! And look at the footprints in the mud!

Queen: Only a giant could make such big footprints.

Oldest Child: Well, I am not afraid of a giant. I will stay out tonight and watch for him. No giant is going to steal from us!

Narrator: The oldest child hid in the garden. She watched as the moon rose. Suddenly, she heard the giant coming. The giant began to take more cabbages.

Oldest Child: Why are you taking our cabbages?

Giant: Why do you ask?

Oldest Child: Those are our cabbages! Leave them alone!

Giant: Well, I won't take them! I will just take you instead!

Narrator: The giant popped the child into his sack, stepped over the wall, and ran to his house. He took the child out of the sack.

Giant: You can get to work. First, take the cow to the field. Then make some porridge.

Narrator: Later, the giant told the child to sit down and eat. Suddenly, she heard a knock at the door.

Oldest Child: Who is there?

From *Multicultural Folktales: Readers Theatre for Elementary Students.* © 2000 Suzanne I. Barchers. Teacher Ideas Press. 1-800-237-6124.

Traveler: I am a weary traveler. I have come a long way and am very hungry. Could you spare some food?

Oldest Child: Go away before the giant finds you. You're not safe here.

Narrator: The child set the porridge on the fire, but then forgot about it. Soon it began to burn.

Giant: You are no use to me! You've burned the porridge! Get into the loft!

Narrator: Meanwhile, the middle child decided to hide in the garden. She hoped that the giant would return. The giant went back to the garden, greedy for more cabbages.

Middle Child: What are you doing in our garden? And what have you done with my sister?

Giant: Aha! Another young one for me. Into the sack with you!

Narrator: The giant took the middle child back to his house. He set her to work, too. Then the middle child heard a knock.

Middle Child: Who is there?

Traveler: I am a weary traveler. I have come a long way and am very hungry. Could you spare some food?

Middle Child: Go away before the giant finds you. You're not safe here.

Narrator: The middle child made a mess of things, too, so the giant sent her into the loft. The children hugged each other, happy to be together again. That night, the giant returned to the garden, where the third child was hiding. But this time his visit was different.

Youngest Child: Good evening, Giant.

Giant: Ha! A polite one! You will come with me.

Youngest Child: I will be glad to. I am ready.

Narrator: The giant put her in the sack on top of the cabbages. She had a small knife with her and cut a hole in the sack so she could watch the way to the house. There the giant set her to work. While she was cooking, she heard a knock.

Traveler: Hello, miss. I am lost and hungry. Can you help me?

Youngest Child: I will give you my dinner. I have had plenty to eat already.

Traveler: Thank you. You've been very kind and I would like to repay you. Let me spin your wool for you.

Narrator: The giant was pleased to see all the work that got done, not realizing that the youngest child had gotten help from the traveler. The giant let her visit with the other children. The next morning, the youngest child started to work again.

Youngest Child: Giant, my mother has no help now. Would you please take her a sack of heather for the cow's bed?

Narrator: The giant decided to help. Soon he was on his way with the basket. The next morning, the third child was hard at work again. She asked for another favor.

Youngest Child: Giant, do you think you could take some grass to my mother? She could use it to feed the cow.

Narrator: The giant took the basket to her mother. The next morning, the youngest child asked another favor.

Youngest Child: Do you think you could take a basket of myrtle to my mother? She would be so happy.

Narrator: The giant agreed again. He didn't notice that the girl was not working when he left. He left the basket by the queen's house. Soon the youngest child slipped out of the basket.

Queen: Thank goodness you are back. You are so clever to have gotten all of us together again!

Middle Child: The giant never knew he was carrying each of us home!

Oldest Child: But what will we do when he finds us gone?

Queen: We won't be here, my children! Let's pack quickly and go.

Narrator: The queen and her children packed as fast as they could. When the giant returned, the house was empty. He rushed back to the garden, but they hadn't even left one cabbage behind. The giant never found them again.

Gifts of Love

Korea

Summary

Before an old woman dies, she gives each of her children her meager possessions. Because the children are so poor, they separate to find better lives. The daughter goes to a cave for the night, where a goblin thinks she is a skeleton. She uses her gourd and walking stick to fool the goblin, going along with him when he steals a prince's soul. The next day, the daughter returns to the kingdom and restores life to the prince. They marry and inherit the throne. She then decides to find her brothers, reuniting their family.

Presentation Suggestions

The daughter has the primary role and should be central on the stage. The mother can leave after her brief lines. The brothers can be on one side of the daughter, with the king and prince on the other side.

Props

The daughter and brothers can be dressed simply. When the daughter marries, she could add an article of clothing or jewelry to indicate her new role. Use artifacts from Korea to enhance the stage.

Delivery Suggestions

The mother should sound weak. The brothers should use normal voices. The daughter should sound timid when dealing with the goblin, but later should plead with the king. The other characters can have normal voices.

Characters

Narrator

Old Woman

Oldest Son

Youngest Son

Daughter

Goblin

King

Prince

Gifts of Love

Narrator: An old woman who lived in Korea was dying. Since her husband had died, the family had been very poor. Still, she had saved a few things for her children. She called her two sons and daughter to her.

Old Woman: My children, I am dying. But I have a few gifts for you. My daughter, I want you to have my walking stick and this bowl. Son, please take this ax. And for you, my youngest son, here is my cooking pot. When I die, I want you to leave this lonely place. Find new lives.

Narrator: Soon the old woman died. Her children buried her and discussed their plans.

Oldest Son: It will be hard to survive here. I think Mother was right when she said we should find new lives.

Youngest Son: But how will we find food? I want to go north, and the way is rugged.

Daughter: I'm not sure where I want to go.

Oldest Son: I think perhaps it would be better if we each went our own way.

Youngest Son: I think that is wise. But I will miss you both.

Daughter: Let's promise to find each other when times are better.

Narrator: And so the young people went away. The daughter walked for a day and decided to spend the night in a cave. When it was dark, she went to sleep. She heard a goblin.

Goblin: Come, skeleton, come with me.

Daughter: Where are you going?

Goblin: What is this? I thought you were dead! Let me feel your skull!

Narrator: The daughter held out the bowl, which was made from a gourd.

Goblin: No hair, so that must be a skull. Let me feel your arm.

Narrator: She held out the walking stick.

Goblin: All right, skeleton, come with me. We are going to snatch the soul of a prince.

Daughter: That should be quite grand! Let's go!

From *Multicultural Folktales: Readers Theatre for Elementary Students.* © 2000 Suzanne I. Barchers. Teacher Ideas Press. 1-800-237-6124.

Narrator: They went together to the nearest palace and sneaked into the prince's room. The goblin stole the prince's soul and put it in a purse. He handed the purse to the daughter to carry. They slipped out of the palace. The next morning, the goblin was gone.

Daughter: Thank goodness the goblin has gone. But he has left the purse with the prince's soul. I had better hurry and take it back to the kingdom.

Narrator: She hurried to the palace and found that everyone was sad. She begged to be allowed to see the king.

King: What do you want, young lady? This is not a good time for us.

Daughter: Your highness, I beg you. Let me have just a moment alone with the body of the prince. I know I can help restore his life. Please let me try.

King: I suppose no harm can come of it. You can have a few minutes, but no more.

Narrator: The daughter entered the prince's room. She closed the door so that she couldn't be seen. Then she slipped over to his bed and opened his mouth. She opened the purse near his mouth. The soul flew right into his mouth, and he came back to life. They went to the king with the news.

Prince: Father, I am well again! This fine young woman gave me back my life!

King: Then we must celebrate!

Narrator: They had a grand party. And as often happens, the two young people fell in love. A wedding soon followed. The marriage was happy, and the couple had a son and a daughter. After some years, the king died, leaving the throne to his son and his wife. One day, the new queen spoke to her husband.

Daughter: My dear, we have a good life. If only I could find my brothers, my happiness would be complete. It has been many years since I have seen them.

Prince: By all means, let us find them. I'll send out messengers to search for them.

Narrator: Before long, a messenger found a farmer who was proved to be the queen's younger brother. She brought her brother back to the court and gave him a position of honor. The messengers continued to search for the old brother. Finally, the queen decided he must be dead. But one day, a slave trader came to court, trying to sell slaves. The queen was about to send him away when she saw one of the slaves.

Daughter: You there, what is your name? Where are you from?

Narrator: The slave was her other brother. He was very sick, but the queen soon nursed him back to health again. He also took a position of honor in the court. The family enjoyed fine lives for many years.

Los Tres Ratoncitos: A Chiste

Southwestern United States

Summary

Tres ratoncitos, three little mice, live with their mother. They want to go out with her to hunt for food, but she wants them to stay safely in their little hole. One day they disobey her, and a cat prepares to eat them. But the mother appears, scaring off the cat by barking like a dog. The story concludes with mother pointing out how useful it is to speak a second language.

Presentation Suggestions

The narrator should stand to one side with the mother mouse next to her. The three mice can be on the other side of the mother mouse.

Props

The stage can be decorated with a stuffed cat and a plate of cheese. A simple mural in the background could depict a mouse hole.

Delivery Suggestions

The three little mice should sound pleading when begging their mother to let them hunt for food. They should sound brave when they decide to go out. The mother mouse should sound firm with them during the first part of the script. Her barking should be convincing. Finally, she should carefully deliver the ending so that the listeners understand the humor in learning a second language.

Characters

Narrator
First Little Mouse
Second Little Mouse
Third Little Mouse
Mother Mouse

"Los Tres Ratoncitos: A Chiste" is adapted from "Los Tres Ratoncitos: A Chiste" in *Una Linda Raza: Cultural and Artistic Traditions of the Hispanic Southwest* (Golden, CO: Fulcrum, 1998), 104. Used with permission.

Los Tres Ratoncitos: A Chiste

Narrator: Once three little mice lived with their mother. They lived in a small hole under a big, fancy house. Every day, the mother mouse would leave the hole. She would search for food for herself and her children.

First Little Mouse: Mama, why can't we go out and look for food?

Second Little Mouse: Please, mama, please!

Third Little Mouse: Yes, Mama. It's boring to sit in our little hole.

Mother Mouse: The world is full of dangers. The big cat is always waiting outside. He would like to catch a nice little mouse and eat him up!

First Little Mouse: Mama, you're just trying to scare us!

Second Little Mouse: We're too smart and fast for any old cat to catch us.

Third Little Mouse: Please let us go!

Mother Mouse: No, you may not go and that's final. Now stay here until I get back. And wish me luck in finding some food for us.

First Little Mouse: Okay, Mama.

Second Little Mouse: We'll stay here.

Third Little Mouse: Good luck, Mama.

Narrator: The mother mouse left. But the mice were not happy.

First Little Mouse: Mama always has such a hard time finding food. Why don't we sneak out and help her?

Second Little Mouse: I know she is trying to protect us. But we're almost grown up.

Third Little Mouse: It's time we started helping out!

First Little Mouse: So we'll sneak out and find some food, right?

Second Little Mouse: We can have it waiting for her when she gets back.

Third Little Mouse: Good idea! Mama will be so proud of us.

Narrator: The three little mice crept out of their hole. They began looking for food. Soon they were lucky. They found some cheese that had been swept into a corner. They tried to carry it back to their hole. They didn't see a big, mean cat sneaking up on them. When they did see the cat, it was too late. The cat trapped them. He was getting ready to eat them!

All Mice: Mama! Mama! Help! Help!

Narrator: Suddenly, the mother mouse leapt between the cat and her baby mice. The cat was ready to pounce on the mother mouse. She reared up on her hind legs and began to bark like a dog!

Mother Mouse: Woof! Woof! Grrr! Woof! Woof!

Narrator: As soon as the cat heard the sound of a dog barking, it turned around and quickly ran away. Later, when the mice were all safe back in their hole, their mother scolded them.

Mother Mouse: Do you see why I asked you to say in the hole?

All Mice: Yes, Mama.

Mother Mouse: One day, you'll be big enough to look for food on your own. There are still many more things you need to learn about the big world outside our hole. And one more thing about the lesson you learned today. *Now* do you see why it's good to know how to speak more than one language?

The Magic Table

Germany

Summary

In this adaptation of a Brothers Grimm folktale, a magic table ensures a lifetime of feasts and thanksgiving. When a father thinks his two sons are not allowing the goat to graze enough, he sends his sons away. After discovering the goat's deceit, the father feels lonely and regretful. The sons' employees give them magic gifts, which they use for their family.

Presentation Suggestions

The father and sons have central roles. Consider having girls read the role of the innkeeper, narrator, and goat to balance out the gender of the characters.

Props

The characters could dress like country folk. Consider adding a table and a club to the stage. The setting should be simple.

Delivery Suggestions

The father should sound angry at first, then regretful, and then happy to have his sons home. The sons should sound more mature after they leave their teachers.

Characters

Narrator
Older Son
Goat
Father
Younger Son
Carpenter
Innkeeper
Woodworker

The Magic Table

 Narrator: Long ago, there was a man who had two sons. He also had one goat. The sons took turns taking the goat out to graze every day. One day, the older son took the goat to the meadow to eat. At the end of the day, he got ready to take the goat home.

Older Son: Goat, have you had enough to eat?

Goat: I'm just so stuffed. I couldn't eat another tuft.

Narrator: So the older son took the goat home.

Father: Son, has the goat had enough to eat?

Older Son: Yes, sir. She was so stuffed that she couldn't eat another tuft!

Narrator: The father decided to check on the goat and went out to the barn.

Father: Goat, have you had enough to eat?

Goat: Enough to eat? Don't make me laugh! I didn't have a single leaf!

Narrator: The father was so mad that he sent his older son away. The next day, he sent his younger son out with the goat. The boy spent a long day with the goat in a garden.

Younger Son: Goat, you have eaten all day. Have you had enough to eat?

Goat: I'm just so stuffed. I couldn't eat another tuft.

Narrator: So the younger son took the goat home.

Father: Son, has the goat had enough to eat?

Younger Son: Yes, sir. She was so stuffed that she couldn't eat another tuft!

Narrator: The father decided to check on the goat and went out to the barn.

Father: Goat, have you had enough to eat?

Goat: Enough to eat? Don't make me laugh! I didn't have a single leaf!

Narrator: The father was so mad that he sent his younger son away. The next morning, he took the goat out to graze.

Father: Let's go, goat. Now you can eat all you want.

Narrator: The father let the goat eat all day. Finally, it was time to go home.

Father: Goat, have you had enough to eat?

Goat: I'm just so stuffed. I couldn't eat another tuft.

Narrator: So the father led the goat home and took her to her stall. As he left, he talked to the goat again.

Father: So, have you *really* had enough to eat?

Goat: Enough to eat? Don't make me laugh! I didn't have a single leaf!

Father: You ungrateful beast! You are a liar! I've sent away my sons because of you! Now I'm all alone!

Narrator: But the man's sons were doing well. The older son had learned to be a carpenter. He worked hard, and his teacher gave him a table as a gift when he was ready to leave.

Carpenter: Young man, you have worked hard. With this table, all you have to do is say, "Table, set yourself." You'll never be hungry again.

Narrator: The man thanked the carpenter and began to travel. After many months, he decided to go home. Perhaps his father would be glad to see him with his magic table. On the way, he stopped at an inn. He asked some men to be his guests, and they all ate well at his magic table.

Innkeeper: That table is amazing! I must have it. While he sleeps, I will trade it for this old one.

Narrator: The next day, the son arrived home. His father was very glad to see him.

Father: Welcome home, my son. What have you been doing?

Older Son: I worked for a carpenter. He gave me this magic table as a gift. Watch this! "Table, set yourself!"

Narrator: But the table did nothing. The older son realized his table had been stolen. Soon he had to go back to work as a carpenter's helper. Meanwhile, the younger son had been working for a woodworker. It came time for him to leave, and the woodworker was sad to see him go.

Woodworker: I have a gift for you. Take this club and carry it in your sack.

Younger Son: Why do I need this club? It will only make my sack heavy.

Woodworker: This is a magic club. If anyone harms you, just say "Club, dance!" The club will dance on the feet of your enemy until you say "Club, get back in the sack."

Narrator: When the younger son returned home, he told his father and brother about his magic club. They decided to put the club to use to get the magic table back. The younger son went to the inn.

Innkeeper: Welcome, young man. I can serve you a fine meal for just one gold coin.

Younger Son: That sounds good to me. I am tired and hungry.

Narrator: The innkeeper gave the younger son a fine dinner, bragging about his magic table.

Younger Son: That was truly a wonderful feast. You are lucky to have such a fine table. But I am lucky, too. My sack contains a treasure I would never give up.

Narrator: The innkeeper decided he had to find out what was in the sack. That night, as the younger son lay sleeping, he sneaked in and slipped the club out of the sack. The younger son was waiting for the innkeeper to do just this.

Younger Son: Club, dance!

Narrator: The club began to dance on the toes of the innkeeper.

Innkeeper: Ow! Ow! Stop this club! I'll give you anything if you will stop it! Ouch! Ouch!

Younger Son: Will you give me the magic table?

Innkeeper: Yes! Ouch! Take it! It's yours!

Younger Son: Club, get back in the sack.

Narrator: So the club stopped dancing on the innkeeper's toes. The younger son took the magic table home. Then the father and his sons sat down to the finest feast they had ever eaten, feeling thankful for their great fortune. The father and his sons enjoyed many years together. And they were never hungry again!

Sally Ann Thunder and Davey Crockett

United States

Summary

Davey Crockett and Mike Fink are swapping tales when a grizzly bear threatens them. Without their rifles, it seems that one of them will surely become the bear's dinner. But Sally Ann Thunder saves Davey Crockett by hitting the bear over the head. Mike and Davey join Sally Ann at the harvest dance, where they meet Sally's friends, Sue and Katy. The new friends share more stories and adventures.

Presentation Suggestions

Although the narrator, Davey, and Mike have more lines than Sally Ann Thunder, Katy, and Sue, the characters' roles are all important. The narrator and men could stand on one side of the stage, with Sally Ann Thunder in the middle, and the women on the other side.

Props

The men could be dressed like frontiersmen. The women could be in country-style dresses or dressed like cowgirls. Davey Crockett could wear a coonskin cap.

Delivery Suggestions

The spoken parts are written in a casual style. The characters should sound folksy. Davey Crockett should sound boastful at times.

Characters

Narrator

Davey Crockett

Mike Fink

Sally Ann Thunder

Katy

Sue

Sally Ann Thunder and Davey Crockett

Narrator: Davey Crockett was born in Tennessee. He loved to hunt. He also loved to tell stories. One day he was walking through the woods with his good friend, Mike Fink.

Davey Crockett: Mike, did I ever tell you the story about the old raccoon that climbed down the tree to meet me?

Mike Fink: No, Davey. Is that how you got your coonskin hat?

Davey Crockett: No, that's a different story.

Mike Fink: Well, you might as well tell me.

Davey Crockett: Well, I was out walking one day, looking to shoot a raccoon. I saw one in a tree and was just about to shoot.

Mike Fink: Why didn't you, Davey?

Davey Crockett: Well, that raccoon looked me straight in the eye and said, "Are you Davey Crockett?" Now I was so surprised that I told him I was.

Mike Fink: Hard to believe that a raccoon was talking to you. But what happened?

Davey Crockett: That old raccoon said, "You don't need to shoot me. I've heard all about you. I'll just come down from the tree right now."

Mike Fink: Did you shoot him then?

Davey Crockett: Heavens-to-Betsy, no! Could you shoot a raccoon who recognized you? I just sent him on his way. Never shot another raccoon again.

Narrator: Davey and Mike walked along, telling stories and lies. Just then, a big old grizzly bear roared at them from behind a nearby tree. Both Davey and Mike were so wrapped up in their tall tales that they weren't paying much attention. Neither of them had his rifle ready.

Mike Fink: Davey, you better run that way. I'll run the other way. One of us will get away.

Narrator: Mike turned and ran, but Davey didn't move fast enough. The old grizzly took one huge paw and pinned Davey right up against a tree. But before that bear could take a taste of Davey, he got hit right alongside the head with a big old stick!

Sally Ann Thunder: Run, you fool!

From *Multicultural Folktales: Readers Theatre for Elementary Students.* © 2000 Suzanne I. Barchers. Teacher Ideas Press. 1-800-237-6124.

Davey Crockett: Yes ma'am! But what about you?

Sally Ann Thunder: Don't worry about me. I'll catch up later.

Narrator: Davey ran off a ways. Before long Mike found him. They walked along, wondering about that gutsy gal. Soon Sally Ann joined them.

Davey Crockett: Well, I owe you a big thanks, ma'am. What did you do about that bear?

Sally Ann Thunder: Oh, that bear and I go way back. I just had to get his attention. Then I could remind him he isn't supposed to be eating humans.

Mike Fink: I'm Mike Fink and this is Davey Crockett. Who might you be?

Sally Ann Thunder: Pleased to meet you. I'm Sally Ann Thunder.

Narrator: The three of them walked along, talking until it was nearly dark. They planned to meet at the harvest dance the next Saturday night. When the time came, they all met at the town square. Sally Ann had brought two friends.

Sally Ann Thunder: Davey Crockett and Mike Fink, I'd like you to meet my best friends, Katy and Sue.

Davey Crockett: How do you do, ladies?

Mike Fink: Hello, Katy and Sue. How do you know Sally Ann?

Katy: Well, Sally Ann saved me from a bear one day. I was cooking dinner and this big old grizzly decided I should be his dinner. But Sally tossed him one of her biscuits.

Davey Crockett: Did the bear decide to eat the biscuits instead?

Sue: No way! That bear took one bite and broke two teeth! It's never bothered anyone since. It just growls and tries to look fierce. Sally Ann calls it "Old Grizzler."

Mike Fink: Now that's some story. But I think that Old Grizzler has bothered at least *one* more person. Right, Davey?

Davey Crockett: Never mind that! Do you have other stories about Sally Ann?

Katy: Well, there was that time she saved Sue.

Mike Fink: What happened?

Sue: It was a pretty summer day. I had taken my best rattlesnake down to the river. We were going to go catfish riding. See, I use my rattlesnake here as reins on that granddaddy catfish.

From *Multicultural Folktales: Readers Theatre for Elementary Students*. © 2000 Suzanne I. Barchers. Teacher Ideas Press. 1-800-237-6124.

Davey Crockett: Why would you be riding a catfish?

Sue: Because it's fun! And I never learned how to swim. That was my problem! I guess my rattlesnake got tired, and it slipped off the catfish. I fell in the river and started to drown. Sally Ann happened to be there. She took one end of that snake and snapped it out over the river. I grabbed it and she pulled me right out of the water!

Narrator: The young people had a grand time that night. They talked and laughed and danced. Finally, the fiddler put away his fiddle. They all started to walk home through the forest. Suddenly, they heard a panther growl. It slipped out from behind a tree.

Davey Crockett: Ladies, let us handle this.

Narrator: First Davey tried to bluff the panther.

Davey Crockett: You're just an overgrown kitten! Now just go on home!

Narrator: But the panther growled even louder.

Mike Fink: Davey, I think we're in trouble here.

Davey Crockett: No, this kitty was just about to leave. Right, kitty cat?

Narrator: The panther growled even louder. Just then, they all heard a different growl.

Sally Ann Thunder: It's Old Grizzler!

Mike Fink: Now we're really in trouble!

Sally Ann Thunder: I don't think so. Just watch.

Narrator: Old Grizzler reared up and roared at that panther. It turned tail and slunk off into the forest. Then Old Grizzler leaned up against an old tree and scratched its back. Davey and Mike walked the ladies home. Everyone said good-night, and Davey and Mike walked toward their cabins.

Davey Crockett: Mike, did I ever tell you about the time I grinned a raccoon right out of a tree?

Mike Fink: No, Davey. But I think you'd better save that story for another time. Let's just get home!

Narrator: That was the end of one story. But it was just the beginning for Sally Ann and Davey Crockett. But that's another story.

The Shepherd and the Troll

Iceland

Summary

Once there was a farmer who raised sheep. Every year on Christmas Eve the troll would come and steal the farmer's shepherd away. Finally, a young boy outsmarts the troll, offering sheep to satisfy his appetite. The third year, the troll takes the boy as well as the sheep. Then the troll befriends the boy, telling him how to find a trade and a wife. When the troll dies, the boy inherits the troll's treasures and lives a long, rich life.

Presentation Suggestions

The narrator, farmer, and boy have the primary roles. The other characters can sit when they are not reading their lines.

Props

The setting can be a simple farm. Consider hanging a mural of a rugged landscape in the background. The students could bring troll dolls to decorate the stage.

Delivery Suggestions

The farmer should sound kindly and concerned about the welfare of his shepherds. The mother should sound worried about her son. The troll should sound fierce and gruff at first and kindly later.

Characters

Narrator
Farmer
Shepherd
Widow
Boy
Troll
Youngest Daughter

The Shepherd and the Troll

Narrator: Once there was a man who lived on a farm. He had many sheep and lived comfortably. He was married, but he had no children. One Christmas Eve the man's shepherd didn't return from tending the sheep. Everyone searched for him, but he was never found. The farmer hired a new shepherd. Soon it was Christmas Eve again.

Farmer: Be careful how you go tonight. Last year my shepherd disappeared on this very night.

Shepherd: Don't worry about me! No one will take me away!

Farmer: Just to be safe, bring the sheep into their pens early. Get back to the farm before dark.

Shepherd: I'll do as you say, but you don't need to worry about me.

Narrator: But just as before, the shepherd disappeared. Meanwhile, there was a poor widow with many children. The farmer went to see her.

Farmer: Ma'am, I came to ask if I could hire your oldest son to watch my sheep.

Widow: He is just a young boy. But we surely could use the money. Let's let him try, and we'll see how it goes.

Narrator: The boy was a good worker, and the farmer grew quite fond of him. The farmer gave him a sheep and a lamb for a gift. But then Christmas Eve came.

Farmer: Son, please be very careful tonight. I beg of you to bring the sheep in early. Then get back to the farm before dark. I don't want to lose another shepherd.

Boy: I'll be careful.

Narrator: The boy watched the sheep all day. When he was about to bring the flock in, he heard heavy footsteps. The boy saw a huge troll coming toward him.

Troll: Good evening! I have come to put you in my bag!

Boy: Oh, no, that wouldn't be wise. Can't you see how thin I am? I have a sheep and lamb here that are so fat. I'll give you them for your pot.

Troll: Give them here, then.

Narrator: The troll took the sheep and lamb and went back up the mountain. The boy went back to the farm.

Farmer: Son, did you see anything unusual tonight?

From *Multicultural Folktales: Readers Theatre for Elementary Students.* © 2000 Suzanne I. Barchers. Teacher Ideas Press. 1-800-237-6124.

Boy: No, everything was about the same.

Narrator: The next day, the farmer was checking his flocks. He saw that the boy's sheep and lamb were missing.

Farmer: Son, what happened to your sheep and lamb?

Boy: A fox killed the lamb. And the sheep fell into a bog. I guess I am not lucky with my own sheep.

Farmer: Son, you have done fine work. I'm going to give you another sheep and lamb. Please stay for another year.

Narrator: The next Christmas Eve, the farmer reminded the boy to be very careful.

Farmer: Son, I hope you'll listen to me. Don't take any risks. Get the sheep back early and come to the farm before dark. It's not safe out there on Christmas Eve.

Boy: Don't worry. There's nothing to fear out there.

Narrator: Later that day, the troll came just as he had before.

Troll: I'm a troll, and tonight you will be put in my pot.

Boy: You can see that I am still very thin. What if I give you two old and two young sheep for your dinner? Will you be satisfied?

Troll: Let me see these sheep.

Narrator: The boy showed him the sheep. The troll threw them over his shoulder and ran away. The boy returned to the farm.

Farmer: Son, did you see anything unusual tonight?

Boy: No, everything was about the same. But I am still unlucky with my sheep.

Narrator: The next summer, the farmer gave the boy four more sheep. When Christmas Eve came, the troll came again.

Troll: Here I am again. This time you won't escape!

Boy: You can see that I am still very thin. What if I give you four fat sheep for your dinner? Will you be satisfied?

Troll: Let me see these sheep.

Narrator: The troll took the sheep over his shoulder, but he also grabbed the boy. The troll ran off to his cave. He told the boy to kill and skin the sheep. The boy soon finished.

Boy: I am all done, troll. Now what do you want me to do?

Troll: Sharpen this ax. I will use it to cut off your head.

Narrator: The boy sharpened the ax and gave it to the troll. But the troll threw down the ax.

Troll: You're a brave lad! I never intended to kill you. You have a good life ahead. Here is what you should do. Next spring, go to the silversmith. Ask to learn the trade. Then take your work to the farm where the three daughters live. The older sisters will admire your work. The youngest won't care, but she is the finest. When you leave, give her this handkerchief, belt, and ring. Then she will fall in love with you. One day you will see me in a dream. Come here and you will find me dead. Bury me. Then take everything of value for yourself.

Narrator: The boy returned to the farm.

Farmer: Son, did you see anything unusual tonight?

Boy: No, everything was about the same.

Narrator: The boy wouldn't answer any more questions. The next spring, he began to learn how to be a silversmith. When the boy had mastered his trade, he took some jewelry he had made to the farm where the three daughters lived. He gave the youngest the handkerchief, the belt, and the ring.

Youngest Daughter: Why are you giving these to me? I should give them back to you.

Narrator: But the boy told her to keep them. After he left, the youngest daughter found that she was in love with him. She told her father, but he wasn't happy about it. But the girl was so sad that she couldn't eat. Finally, the father agreed to the engagement.

Before long, the boy dreamed that the troll had died. He took both the farmers with him to help. When they got there, the troll was dead. They buried the troll and gathered all the treasures. Soon after, the boy married the youngest daughter. They lived long and full lives, just as the troll had said they would.

Spider Flies to the Feast

Liberia

Summary

In this story from the Dan ethnic group, Spider plays many tricks on Dog. When Dog almost bites off Spider's leg, he quits playing tricks for a while. But when the Great Spirit has a feast for the birds, Spider can't resist making wings and flying to the feast. When he tricks the birds out of their food, they retaliate and Spider has a nearly tragic fall to earth.

Presentation Suggestions

The narrator should stand to one side, with Dog next, followed by Spider. The other characters should stand on the other side of Spider because they read during the second half of the script.

Props

The stage could be decorated with African artifacts. A mural could display a variety of birds. Each character could wear a simple sign showing the name of that character.

Delivery Suggestions

Spider should sound boastful and confident. Dog should sound disbelieving during many of his lines. When Spider tricks them, the birds should sound outraged. The Great Spirit should sound benevolent and powerful.

Characters

Narrator
Spider
Dog
Eagle
Great Spirit
Quail
Hummingbird

"Spider Flies to the Feast" was adapted from "Spider Flies to the Feast" in *Why Leopard Has Spots: Dan Stories from Liberia* by Won-Ldy Paye and Margaret H. Lippert, illustrated by Ashley Bryan (Golden, CO: Fulcrum, 1998), 23–30. Used with permission.

Spider Flies to the Feast

Narrator: Spider and Dog were friends. Every day Spider would float downriver to visit Dog. But he always had to walk home. No one could swim upstream against the swift current. Spider loved to play tricks on Dog.

Spider: I have a new trick. I can go home without walking on the ground! Can you do that?

Dog: No, and neither can you.

Spider: Yes, I can. I can walk in space.

Dog: Ha! Nobody can walk in space.

Spider: Nobody *except* me.

Dog: Prove it.

Narrator: Spider climbed to the top of Dog's house. He let out a silky thread so thin that Dog couldn't see it. Then he waved one leg.

Dog: Let go. You aren't walking through space. Anybody can wave a leg out in space.

Narrator: Spider waved another leg, and another, and another. He was waiting for the wind.

Dog: Let go with all your legs.

Narrator: The wind came up. It blew the end of the thread toward Spider's house, and the thread caught on Spider's roof. Then Spider stepped off Dog's roof onto the thread and began to walk.

Dog: How do you do that? I never saw anybody walk in space before.

Narrator: Spider walked all the way to his house while Dog followed. Then he climbed down and grinned.

Spider: Did you like my trick?

Dog: You were lucky, Spider. You could have crashed and hurt yourself. Tricks can really get you in trouble. So from now on, no more tricks.

Narrator: Dog wagged his tail good-bye and jumped into the river. He floated home with the current. The next day, Spider floated downriver to see Dog again.

Spider: I have a better trick. I can get home without walking on the ground or walking in space.

Dog: How?

Spider: On the river.

Dog: The current is too fast. No one can go upriver.

Spider: I can.

Dog: Prove it.

Narrator: Spider took a deep breath and plunged into the river. He sank below the surface. Dog bounded to the edge of the riverbank to rescue his friend. He stopped short as Spider's head bobbed up.

Spider: Watch carefully.

Narrator: Spider began moving all eight legs at once, very fast. He was skating on the surface of the water. Gradually he worked his way upstream. Dog was amazed. He raced up the path and waited by Spider's house. Soon Spider skated to the bank and climbed out.

Spider: Did you like my new trick?

Dog: How did you do that? I never saw anybody walk on water before. That's dangerous, Spider. You could have drowned. I told you that tricks can really get you in trouble. So no more tricks. I'm going home.

Spider: Tomorrow, I will come visit you without walking on the ground, without walking in space, and without skating on the river.

Narrator: When Dog got to his house, he waded out of the river and shook himself dry. Then he sat down and scratched his belly.

Dog: That Spider! What will he do next?

Narrator: Early the next morning, Spider cooked a huge pumpkin, cut off the lid, scooped out the seeds, spiced it up, climbed inside, and pulled the lid shut.

Spider: Soon Dog will get tired of waiting for me. He'll come looking for me, and when he sees this yummy pumpkin he'll carry it back to his house, with me inside it!

Narrator: Spider was so excited he could hardly sit still. Dog waited and waited for Spider.

Dog: I wonder what happened to Spider. Maybe this time his trick got him in trouble. Maybe he's hurt. I had better go look for him.

Narrator: Dog trotted up the path to look for Spider. As he got close to Spider's house, he smelled something delicious.

Dog: Mmmm. Lunchtime. Why, that pumpkin is enough food for both of us. Spider! Where are you?

Narrator: Spider heard Dog, but he didn't answer. He was waiting until Dog got the pumpkin back to his house. Meanwhile, Dog decided to take a taste of the pumpkin. He sank his teeth into the pumpkin and bit Spider's leg.

Spider: Ouch!

Narrator: Dog heard Spider. He thought he must be hurt. But before going to look for him he took another bite from the pumpkin. He almost bit off Spider's leg.

Spider: Stop biting me!

Narrator: Spider crawled out of the pumpkin, rubbing his leg.

Dog: What were you doing in there?

Spider: Waiting for you to carry me to your house!

Dog: *That* was your trick?

Spider: Yes.

Dog: That was really stupid. I could have eaten you up by accident. I told you that tricks can get you in trouble!

Spider: All right, Dog. From now on, no more tricks.

Narrator: For many months, Spider remembered what he had said to Dog. Of course, he kept thinking of great tricks, but he didn't play them on anybody. Then the dry season came. Spider swung lazily from a thread, trying to catch a breeze. Spider saw Eagle stretch her wings and soar high in the sky. Eagle called to the other birds.

Eagle: It's cool up here! Come on up!

Narrator: Spider watched the birds swoop through the air. The Great Spirit looked down fondly as the birds flew in circles and flitted about. She spoke to them.

Great Spirit: I would like to reward you for entertaining me. Come to my house to-morrow for a feast.

Narrator: Spider heard the Great Spirit. He waved his legs, thinking that he was just as good as the birds. After all, he had eight legs and they had only two. But no one was watching.

Spider: I know! I'll make my own wings and fly to the feast myself.

Narrator: Spider went to Quail's house to ask for some feathers.

Spider: Quail, do you have some extra feathers around?

Quail: You can have the ones over there in the grass.

Narrator: Then Spider asked Eagle for feathers.

Spider: Eagle, could I borrow some feathers?

Eagle: Take the ones on the ground below my nest.

Narrator: Spider gathered big feathers from Vulture, Woodpecker, and Blue Heron. Then he gathered small feathers from Pepper Bird, Parrot, and Hummingbird. Soon he had a huge pile of feathers. He arranged them on the ground in the shape of a coat with wings. He scraped the bark of a rubber tree until sticky white gum seeped out. He spread it on the feathers. When the glue was dry, he put on his new coat and flapped his wings. His wings flopped back and forth. He bumped along the ground and then took off. In a few moments he was flying.

Spider: I'm flying! I'm flying! Wait till the birds see this!

Narrator: The next morning, the birds woke up early. They started flying to the feast. Spider woke up late. He poked his head out of his door and saw them high in the sky.

Spider: Hey! Wait for me!

Narrator: Spider put on his coat and began to fly after them. He flew all morning. He followed the birds into the clouds. His legs ached. His back hurt. And he was hungry. Finally, he arrived at the feast. He slipped inside. The Great Spirit was talking.

Great Spirit: Welcome. I hope you all enjoy the feast. This is the first time you have been together, so I would like you to introduce yourselves.

Eagle: My name is Eagle.

Quail: My name is Quail.

Hummingbird: My name is Hummingbird.

Spider: My name is All of You.

Narrator: The birds all introduced themselves. Then the Great Spirit said it was time to eat. Hummingbird flitted over to a bright red hibiscus. Parrot cracked some sunflower seeds. Pepper Bird plucked a sweet pepper from a vine.

Spider: Wait! Great Spirit, who is this feast for?

Great Spirit: This feast is for all of you.

Spider: Wow! This feast is just for me, because my name is All of You. You can't eat any of my food!

Narrator: He snatched the food from the birds. They shrieked and honked, but Spider was fast. In a flash all the food was gone. The Great Spirit saw that the birds were angry. Spider will be sorry, she thought. When it was time to leave, Eagle spoke to Hummingbird.

Eagle: Those feathers on All of You look a lot like yours.

Hummingbird: Yes, they *are* mine. And those long feathers on his wings look a lot like yours. All of You must really be Spider.

Spider: Whoops! I think I heard my name. I'd better go now.

Narrator: Spider took off for home. Eagle soared after him.

Eagle: Spider, you tricked us! I want my feathers back.

Spider: Oh, sure. I have plenty more.

Narrator: Spider broke off Eagle's feathers and gave them to him. Then the other birds took back their feathers. Soon Spider flapped his legs, but he began to fall. Just then, Hummingbird flew by.

Spider: Help me, little Hummingbird. Hurry down to earth. Tell my family to cover the ground under me with soft leaves.

Narrator: But Hummingbird remembered what Spider had done. She was hungry, and she knew her friends were, too. She sped down to earth and called to his family.

Hummingbird: Spider has a new trick he wants to show you. Bring thorny branches and stick them in the ground with the points straight up. Spider will stop just above them.

Narrator: Spider's family was used to his tricks. They did just as Hummingbird said. Spider fell through the clouds. He heard everybody cheering him. He saw the thorny branches.

Spider: What is the matter with you? Where are the soft leaves? Why are there thorns?

Narrator: Thowk! Poor Spider lay on the thorns. He could hardly move. The only thing that saved his life was the hard glue from the bird-feather coat. All his legs were broken. That's why his legs are crooked. Spider still loves to fly, but he has never again tried to make wings. Now he has to wait for the wind so that he can sail through the air on his silken thread.

Chapter 3

Third-Grade Reading Level

 The Clever Daughter

Italy

 Dick Whittington and His Cat

England

 Finding the Foolish

Scotland

 The Master-Maid

Norway

 The Tree That Bled Fish

Micronesia

 Water, Water Will Be Mine

Kenya

The White-Haired Old Woman

United States, Native American

Why Ants Carry Burdens

Africa/Hausa

The Clever Daughter

Italy

Summary

A peasant and his daughter discover a gold mortar while farming. The peasant insists on giving it to the king. The peasant's daughter warns her father that the king will suspect they also found a pestle. As she predicted, the peasant is imprisoned when the king doesn't believe him. The king challenges the peasant's daughter to solve a riddle, offering his hand in marriage if she succeeds. The king and the daughter marry, but once again, the daughter must prove her wisdom through her devotion to her husband.

Presentation Suggestions

The narrator, peasant, and daughter should stand to one side. The king should stand in the middle, with the other characters on the other side of the king.

Props

The stage could be enhanced with farming implements and plants behind the peasant and his daughter. The other side of the stage could resemble the inside of a palace, with fancy chairs or decorations. The characters can dress according to their roles.

Delivery Suggestions

The father should sound distressed while in the prison. The king should sound regal. The daughter should sound wise and patient.

Characters

Narrator
Daughter
Father
King
First Peasant
Second Peasant

The Clever Daughter

Narrator: Once there was a peasant who lived in a small house with his daughter. One day, the daughter came to her father with an idea.

Daughter: Father, I think we should ask the king for some land to farm.

Father: That's a good idea, dear. We could improve our lives with just a bit of land for ourselves.

Narrator: The daughter wasted no time in going to the king. Seeing how poor they were, the king granted the daughter's request. One day, the father and daughter were spading the land when they found a mortar of pure gold.

Father: Dear, the king was so good to give us this land. Let's give him this mortar we have found.

Daughter: But Father, if we give him a mortar and no pestle, he'll think we are keeping the pestle. I think we should just keep quiet.

Father: I disagree. I am going to give the mortar to the king.

Narrator: The father went to see the king.

Father: Your majesty, while spading my farmland, my daughter and I found this mortar. You were kind to us, giving us the land. Now I would like to give you this gift.

King: Did you find anything else?

Father: No, this was all.

King: What about the pestle? If there is a mortar, there must be a pestle!

Father: Sir, this is all we found. Please believe me.

King: I don't believe you. Off to the prison with you until you decide to give me the pestle.

Narrator: The father realized all too late that his daughter had been right. While he was in his cell, he sighed and talked to himself.

Father: If only I had listened to my daughter! If only I had listened to my daughter!

Narrator: The servants told the king how the peasant kept sighing. The father wouldn't eat or drink either. Finally, the king went to talk with the peasant.

King: Why do you keep sighing?

Father: Oh, if only I had listened to my daughter.

King: Why? What did she tell you?

Father: She told me not to give you the mortar. She said you would only want the pestle as well.

King: Well, if your daughter is so clever, tell her I want to see her.

Narrator: The next time the daughter came to visit her father, he told her to go see the king.

King: Your father says that you are very clever. I have a riddle for you to solve. If you succeed, I will marry you.

Daughter: I would like that very much, Your Majesty. What is the riddle?

King: Here is the riddle. Come to me not clothed, not naked, not riding, not walking, not on the road, and not off the road. If you can do that, I will marry you.

Daughter: I will be back, Your Majesty.

Narrator: The peasant's daughter went home. She took off all her clothes and wrapped herself in a big fishnet. Then she hired a donkey and tied the fishnet to its tail. The donkey dragged her along. She wasn't walking or riding. As he dragged her along, she touched her big toes to the ground so that she was neither on the road nor off it. Soon she came to the king.

Daughter: As you can see, Your Majesty, I have solved your riddle.

King: Indeed you have. I'll let your father out of prison, and we can plan our marriage.

Narrator: As was the custom, the king put his new bride in charge of all his household and royal possessions. They had a happy married life. One day, two peasants sought the king's counsel.

First Peasant: Your Majesty, my foal ran off and lay down between two oxen harnessed to this man's wagon. I want my foal back. After all, it belongs to me.

Second Peasant: But you lost control of your foal. Therefore, the foal is mine.

King: Since the foal ran to your oxen, you may indeed keep it.

Narrator: The peasant left, weeping about the loss of his foal. He had heard that the queen was wise and kindhearted. He decided to go to her with his problem. She listened carefully before she spoke to him.

Daughter: If you promise to keep this a secret, I will tell you what to do.

First Peasant: Of course, I will never share what I have learned from you.

Daughter: Tomorrow morning, when the king goes out to inspect his troops, take a fishnet and stand in the middle of the road. Pretend that you are fishing. Shake out the net now and then as if it were full. Then continue to pretend to be fishing.

From *Multicultural Folktales: Readers Theatre for Elementary Students.* © 2000 Suzanne I. Barchers. Teacher Ideas Press. 1-800-237-6124.

Narrator: After telling the peasant what to say if the king questioned him, the daughter told him to go on his way. The next morning the peasant stood fishing on dry land. The king came by on his way to inspect the troops.

King: What are you doing?

First Peasant: Your Majesty, I am fishing.

King: How can you be fishing on dry land?

First Peasant: There is just as much chance of my catching a fish on dry land as there is of an ox having a foal.

King: You didn't think of this yourself. Who told you to be so clever and bold?

First Peasant: No one helped me, sir.

Narrator: The king refused to believe him and had the peasant beaten. Finally, he confessed that the queen had told him what to say. The king went to his wife.

King: Why have you been untrue to me? You counseled this peasant behind my back. I won't have you for my wife any longer. Go back to the peasant life you came from.

Daughter: I understand that I have displeased you, but may I have one last request?

King: What would that be?

Daughter: I would like to take along the dearest farewell gift I can think of.

King: I guess that would be acceptable.

Daughter: Then if that is your command, I will obey it.

Narrator: She threw her arms around him and asked him to have a farewell drink with her. She secretly slipped a sleeping potion in the drink. While he was sleeping, she called a servant and wrapped a fine white sheet around him. Then she had the servant carry him to a carriage. She took him home to her little house. When a day and a night had passed, the king woke up.

King: Where am I? Where are my servants?

Daughter: Dear husband, you told me to take what was dearest with me. Nothing is dearer to me than you. So I took you with me.

King: Dear wife, you are truly wise. We shall never part again. Let's go home.

Narrator: The king and his wife returned to the royal palace. From that day forward, the king's wife helped the king with many decisions in the court. In fact, I think they are still together, even now.

Dick Whittington and His Cat

England

Summary

Dick Whittington found himself a poor orphan and went to seek his fortune in London. He found a job in a kitchen, sleeping in a rat-infested garret. Using a penny, he purchased a cat, who eventually went on a ship to Barbary. The king of Barbary exchanged a great treasure for the cat so that he could rid his court of rats. Dick found himself a wealthy young man with a fine future.

Presentation Suggestions

Dick and the narrator have the primary roles. They can both be toward the front, with Dick in the center. Mr. Fitzwarren should also have a prominent position. The gentleman could exit or sit down after his lines. Alice should stand next to Mr. Fitzwarren. The captain, king, queen, and merchant could be grouped together to one side.

Props

Dick should be dressed in poor clothes. The cook can be wearing an apron. Mr. Fitzwarren and Alice should be well dressed. The king and queen can be dressed in robes to symbolize royalty. A toy cat could be placed onstage.

Delivery Suggestions

Dick should sound somewhat timid and quiet. The cook should sound cruel. Mr. Fitzwarren should sound kind and fair. The others should have normal delivery, appropriate to their roles.

Characters

Narrator
Dick
Gentleman
Cook
Mr. Fitzwarren
Alice
Captain
King
Queen
Merchant

From *Multicultural Folktales: Readers Theatre for Elementary Students.* © 2000 Suzanne I. Barchers. Teacher Ideas Press. 1-800-237-6124.

Dick Whittington and His Cat

Narrator: Long ago in England, there lived a young boy named Dick Whittington. His father and mother died when he was very young. Dick was too young to work, so he had little to eat. Dick decided he had to take fate into his own hands.

Dick: I have heard that people are grand in London. Fine ladies and gentlemen sing all day long. I've even heard that the streets are paved with gold! I think I will go there.

Narrator: Dick saw a large wagon with eight horses. He thought this wagon must be going to London. He asked the driver if he could walk alongside the wagon, and after much walking he arrived in London safely. As soon as he arrived, he ran off, hoping to find his fortune. Soon he realized that the streets were not paved with gold. Night came. Dick found a corner and cried himself to sleep. The next morning, he asked strangers for help.

Dick: Could you spare a penny? I'm hungry and have nowhere to go.

Gentleman: I won't give you any money. You should get work, young man.

Dick: I would work, but I don't know how to get work.

Gentleman: If you really want to work, come with me. There is a nearby hay field that needs working.

Narrator: Dick worked hard, living well until the hay was in. Then he went to the home of Mr. Fitzwarren, a rich merchant. The cook saw him hanging about.

Cook: What are you doing out there?

Dick: Nothing, ma'am.

Cook: Well, if you are here to beg, you might as well be gone. If you don't leave soon, I'll be pouring these slops on you.

Narrator: Just then, Mr. Fitzwarren came home and saw Dick.

Mr. Fitzwarren: What are you doing hanging about, boy? You look old enough to work.

Dick: I would happily work. But I don't know anyone to give me work. I am nearly faint from hunger.

Mr. Fitzwarren: Let me take you to the cook. She can feed you and put you to work.

Narrator: Dick would have been happy with this work, except for the cook. She scolded him and shook her ladle at him.

Cook: Look sharp! Clean the spit! Then make the fire. Scrub the floor. And waste no time, you scoundrel.

Narrator: Dick tolerated her as best he could. But his room was another matter. His bed was in a garret, where the floor had many holes. Every night rats and mice crawled about his room. Dick decided to take a penny he had saved and buy a cat. Dick bought a fine cat and soon had no trouble with rats. One day, Mr. Fitzwarren called everyone together.

Mr. Fitzwarren: My ship is ready to sail. Do you have a few coins you wish to send with me? I will do my best to bring you a fine profit.

Narrator: All the others had a few coins to risk. But Dick had nothing to spare. Mr. Fitzwarren's daughter, Alice, offered to share some of her own money with Dick.

Alice: I will give you some money for Dick, Father.

Mr. Fitzwarren: No, my dear. Dick must give something of his own.

Dick: All I have is a cat.

Mr. Fitzwarren: Then fetch your cat! Let her go. Perhaps she will bring you luck.

Narrator: Dick did so sadly, knowing he faced more mice and rats. Alice felt sorry for him.

Alice: Dick, here is a penny. Buy yourself another cat.

Dick: Thank you, Alice. I will be grateful for another cat.

Narrator: But Alice's kindness only caused the cook to be jealous of Dick. She began to treat him with more cruelty.

Cook: You foolish boy! Sending your cat to sea! Do you think you will get anything back? Ha! Just keep scrubbing those pans. Then mop the floor.

Narrator: Dick decided he couldn't bear life under her rule any longer. He packed up his few things and went a ways away before he stopped to rest. He heard the bells of Bow Church and they seemed to speak to him, saying, "Turn again, Whittington, Thrice Lord Mayor of London."

Dick: Lord Mayor of London! Why, I could put up with anything if I am someday going to be Lord Mayor of London! I'll go back and put up with the bad temper of the cook.

Narrator: Meanwhile, the ship had landed on the coast of Barbary, where the people came to buy fine things. The captain visited the king and queen, but just as they were about to sit down to dinner, rats and mice rushed in and ate all the meat!

Captain: Your Majesty, how can you put up with all these rats?

King: It is terrible, but I don't know what to do. I would give a fine treasure to be rid of them.

Captain: I believe I can help you. I have an animal on board that would destroy these creatures in no time.

Queen: Oh, please, Captain. Please fetch her for us!

King: If you can truly do this, I will load your ship with gold and jewels in exchange for her.

Captain: Without her, my ship will be taken over with rats. But I will bring her to you.

Narrator: The captain brought the cat, and she made short work of many of the rats. The rest fled to their holes. The king and queen were delighted.

Queen: Bring that dear animal to me!

Narrator: The queen stroked the cat, and the cat purred herself to sleep. The king, seeing that the cat would soon have kittens, bargained for treasures for the whole ship. Then he gave the captain a fortune for the cat. The captain loaded his ship and set sail for London, arriving without further trouble. One day, Mr. Fitzwarren was in his office when someone knocked on his door.

Mr. Fitzwarren: Who's there?

Merchant: I come bringing you news of your ship.

Mr. Fitzwarren: Tell me. What have you heard?

Merchant: The voyage has been very prosperous. The ship is full of riches. Also, in Barbary, the king's court was overrun with rats, and the captain gave a fortune in exchange for Dick's cat.

Mr. Fitzwarren: Well, we must fetch young Dick right away!

Merchant: You are going to give a servant such riches?

Mr. Fitzwarren: Of course! It is his own doing, and he shall have every penny.

Narrator: Mr. Fitzwarren sent for Dick and told him to sit down.

Dick: Sir, if you please. I cannot sit among such fine men. Let me return to the kitchen.

Merchant: Mr. Whittington, we welcome you here. The captain sold your cat to the king of Barbary. His court was overrun with mice, and he sent you a treasure in return. We all congratulate you on your good fortune!

Dick: Please, Mr. Fitzwarren, take some of this for your kindness to me.

Mr. Fitzwarren: No, Dick. It is all yours!

Narrator: Dick tried to share some of his treasure with Alice, but she would not take any. He made a present to the captain, the mate, Mr. Fitzwarren's servants, and even the old cook. Then Mr. Fitzwarren helped Dick find a tailor and groom himself. Mr. Fitzwarren let Dick live in his house while he learned how to live like a gentleman. Soon Dick's friendship with Alice grew and they decided to marry. A fine wedding was held. Dick Whittington and Alice lived in fine splendor. Dick even became sheriff and eventually became Lord Mayor of London— three times! And, of course, the Whittingtons' favorite pet was always a cat!

From *Multicultural Folktales: Readers Theatre for Elementary Students.* © 2000 Suzanne I. Barchers. Teacher Ideas Press. 1-800-237-6124.

Finding the Foolish

Scotland

Summary

When a young wife notices a saddle hanging above her head in the stable, she decides she easily could have been killed. Her mother and father join her, lamenting what might have happened. Her husband decides they are all foolish and leaves in search of three other foolish people. Three wives in a nearby town compete to show just how foolish their husbands can be. In the traditional ending, the prize goes to the wife who convinces her husband that he is dead. In this version, the audience is asked to determine which husband was the most foolish.

Presentation Suggestions

There are many characters in this play. Young Wife, Mother, and Father may wish to sit down after their parts. The three wives and husbands could be paired on the stage. Have the wives step forward for their parts when they are in the cottage. Each couple should step forward as they converse and step back when they are finished. Have the three husbands step forward for the end.

Props

The women could be dressed in dresses and aprons. The first and second husbands could be in work clothes. The third husband could be in a nightshirt.

Delivery Suggestions

Young Wife, Father, and Mother should sound sad and worried. The husbands should sound sensible. The three wives should sound persuasive when talking to their husbands.

Characters

Narrator
Young Wife
Mother
Father
Young Husband
First Wife
Second Wife
Third Wife
First Husband
Second Husband
Third Husband

Finding the Foolish

Narrator: A young wife and her husband lived at her parents' farm. They were happy, working together at their chores. After a morning of work, the young wife went home to feed the horses and collect the family's dinner. When she went into the stable, she noticed the mare's saddle hanging on the wall above her head.

Young Wife: Oh, dear! If this saddle were to fall on my head, I would be killed!

Narrator: The young wife sat down and began to cry at the thought of dying so young. Meanwhile, her family was getting hungry as they worked in the fields. Her mother decided to return to the farm and look for her. She found the young wife weeping in the stable.

Mother: Whatever is the matter? Why are you weeping?

Young Wife: I came in here to feed the horses and saw the saddle above my head. I realized that if it had fallen I would be killed. The thought of that made me sad.

Mother: You are right, my dear! It surely would have killed you! And what would I have done without my daughter?

Narrator: The mother sat down and began crying with her daughter. The father, beginning to wonder if something had happened to the women, came looking for them. He found them in the stable.

Father: What is wrong? Why are you both weeping?

Mother: Oh, husband! When I came in I found our daughter in tears. She saw the saddle above and began to think how terrible it would be if it were to fall and she were killed.

Father: That indeed would have been tragic!

Narrator: And the father sat down and began to cry at the thought of his daughter dying. Finally, the young husband came searching for them and found them all in the stable.

Young Husband: Why are you all crying in the stable? What has happened?

Father: When your wife came into the stable, she saw the saddle above her head. She realized that if it had fallen, she would have died. We are all upset by the thought.

Young Husband: Well, this is foolish! The saddle didn't fall, and my wife is just fine. Let's go get our dinner.

From *Multicultural Folktales: Readers Theatre for Elementary Students.* © 2000 Suzanne I. Barchers. Teacher Ideas Press. 1-800-237-6124.

Narrator: The next day, the husband got to thinking about how foolish his family had been. He made a surprising announcement to them.

Young Husband: I will be gone for a while. I am going to try to find three more people as foolish as you.

Narrator: The young husband set out for the next village. Soon he came to a cottage with its door wide open. He could see some women spinning in the front room.

Young Husband: Are you from the town?

First Wife: We did not come from the town, but we are married to some men who did.

Young Husband: Is the town a good place to live?

Second Wife: It is good enough.

Third Wife: But our men are so foolish that we can make them believe anything.

Young Husband: I would like to see that. I'll give this gold ring to the woman who can make her husband look the most foolish.

Narrator: The women were eager to show the young husband just how foolish their husbands could be and invited him to stay and watch the fun. When the first woman's husband came home from work that day, she began her plan.

First Wife: Dear, you look terribly sick today.

First Husband: I do?

First Wife: Oh, yes, dear. I think you had better take off your clothes and get into bed.

Narrator: The man took off his clothes and got into bed, thinking he must look awful.

First Wife: You look near dead!

First Husband: I do? What can be happening? I felt quite well this morning!

First Wife: Oh, dear! What am I going to do? He's dead!

Narrator: She reached over and closed his eyes. The husband decided he must indeed be dead. Meanwhile, the second husband came home.

Second Wife: What is going on here? You are not my husband!

Second Husband: What do mean? I am most certainly your husband!

Second Wife: No, it isn't you at all. Be off with you.

Narrator: So the second husband went to sleep in the woods. Early the next morning, a messenger came to tell the third husband that he needed to attend the burial of the first husband. He began to get up, but his wife told him not to hurry. Soon the funeral procession began to pass by.

From *Multicultural Folktales: Readers Theatre for Elementary Students.* © 2000 Suzanne I. Barchers. Teacher Ideas Press. 1-800-237-6124.

Third Wife: Now you must hurry. We must leave now or we shall be late.

Third Husband: But where are my clothes?

Third Wife: Husband! You are wearing them! Let's go! We don't want to miss the burial.

Third Husband: Are you sure? It doesn't feel as though I'm wearing my clothes.

Narrator: But the man listened to his wife, and off they went with him dressed only in his nightshirt. When the mourners saw him, they ran away in fright. The third husband stood by the coffin, looking at the first husband. Then the second husband came out of the woods, looking rumpled and exhausted.

Third Husband: Why do you look as though you've had no sleep?

Second Husband: Because I am not who I am. But why are you in your nightshirt?

Third Husband: I am not! My wife told me I had on all my clothes.

Narrator: Suddenly, the first husband sat up in the coffin.

First Husband: And my wife told me that I was dead!

Narrator: The second and third husbands were so terrified they ran all the way home. The third husband got out of the coffin and went home. And now, dear audience, we leave it to you to decide. Only one wife will get the gold ring. Which husband was the most foolish?

The Master-Maid

Norway

Summary

A prince decides to travel the world. He takes a job with a giant, but discovers that the giant is evil. The giant's master-maid helps the prince with her magic, and they escape together. When the prince returns to his kingdom, he doesn't follow the master-maid's directions and loses his memory of her. Meanwhile, the master-maid uses her magic to outwit several would-be suitors. Eventually, all events converge to bring the master-maid to the palace, where the prince finally realizes she is his true love.

Presentation Suggestions

This is a long story, with an especially long role for the narrator. The narrator should have a prominent place onstage, along with the prince and the master-maid. The giant, guard, and drop of blood could exit or sit down after their lines. The sheriff, attorney, and bailiff could enter when their turns come.

Props

Items made of gold appear several times in the story. Props that look like gold could decorate the stage. Large pots could represent the cauldrons. The giant could dress in large clothing and boots to appear big. The prince could be dressed in good but not regal clothing.

Delivery Suggestions

The giant should sound threatening and gruff. The sheriff, attorney, and bailiff should sound conniving. Although the story does not specify their motivations, they are greedy, and this could be emphasized by their voices. The other characters should speak with normal voices.

Characters

Narrator
Giant
Prince
Master-Maid
Guard
Drop of Blood
Sheriff
Attorney
Bailiff

The Master-Maid

Narrator: Once upon a time, there was a king who had many sons. The youngest prince decided to go into the world and try his luck. He traveled for several days and came to a giant's house, where he asked for work. The giant hired him.

Giant: I am going to take the goats to pasture. While I am gone, you must clean out the stable. That will be enough work for one day. You'll find that I am a kind master, but I expect you to do your work well. And don't go into any rooms beyond where you sleep at night. If you do, I will have to take your life.

Prince: That sounds fair. I'll get right to work on the stable.

Narrator: The prince started working, but he couldn't stop thinking about the forbidden rooms.

Prince: He is an easy master. But it would be interesting to look into those other rooms. He must be afraid I'll see something. Well, he'll never know if I take just a peek.

Narrator: The prince sneaked into the first room. A cauldron hanging from the wall was boiling, but the prince could see no fire under it.

Prince: I wonder what is inside the cauldron.

Narrator: The prince dipped a lock of hair in the cauldron, and it came out as if it were made of copper. He went into the next room and found another boiling cauldron. He thrust another lock of hair in it, and it came out as if it were made of silver. In a third room, he found another cauldron; this time, the prince's lock of hair was turned to gold.

Prince: These are remarkable cauldrons. What could be in the fourth room?

Narrator: In the next room, he found no cauldron, but seated on a bench was a beautiful young woman.

Master-Maid: What are you doing here?

Prince: I came to work for the giant.

Master-Maid: I hope you find a better place soon!

Prince: But he seems like a kind enough master. The work isn't hard. Once I clean out the stable, I'll be done for the day.

Master-Maid: I see you haven't started yet. You'll soon discover that ten pitchforks-full will come for every one you throw out. But here is what you must do to succeed. Turn your pitchfork upside down and work with the handle. Everything will fly out by itself.

Prince: Thank you! I'll do just that.

Narrator: But the prince stayed for most of the day, getting to know the young lady. Finally, it got to be late in the day.

Master-Maid: You should leave now. You still have the stable to clean out.

Narrator: The prince left and began to work in the usual way. But the stable filled up with every toss of the pitchfork. He decided to try the method the master-maid had told him. In the twinkling of an eye the stable was clean. The prince returned to his room shortly before the giant returned with his goats.

Giant: Have you cleaned the stable?

Prince: Yes, master, it is sweet and clean.

Giant: Well, I shall see about that.

Narrator: The giant went to the stable and knew that the prince must have had some help.

Giant: You must have been talking to my master-maid. You never could have known how to clean out the stable without her help.

Prince: Master-maid? What is a master-maid? I would like to see that.

Giant: Well, you'll see soon enough!

Narrator: The next morning, the giant told the prince about his next chore.

Giant: Today you must fetch my horse. It's on the mountainside. When you are done, you may rest, for I am a kind master. But don't go into any of the forbidden rooms. If you do, I will wring your head off.

Narrator: Of course, the prince could not resist going to see the master-maid again.

Master-Maid: What is your work today?

Prince: Today's work is easy. All I have to do is go up the mountainside and get the giant's horse.

Master-Maid: How do you plan to do that?

Prince: How hard can it be? I'll simply catch the horse and ride it back.

Master-Maid: It won't be all that easy. But here is what to do. When you get near the horse, fire will burst out of its nostrils. Be very careful and take the bridle hanging by the door over here. Fling the bit straight into its jaws. Then it will become so tame that you will be able to ride it.

Narrator: The prince and the master-maid spent the day talking of one thing and another. Soon they found themselves falling in love and talking of marriage. Finally, it grew late, so the prince took the bridle and caught the horse easily. He brought it back to the stable. Later that evening, the giant came home.

Giant: Have you brought home the horse?

Prince: Yes, sir. And what an amusing horse to ride! He's in the stable.

Giant: You have been talking with my master-maid again, haven't you? You never could have ridden that horse without her advice.

Prince: Master, you keep talking about a master-maid. What is this thing? I would love to see it.

Giant: You'll see soon enough!

Narrator: On the morning of the third day, the giant prepared to leave again.

Giant: Today you must go underground and fetch my taxes. When you are done, you may rest for the day. You'll see just what an easy master I am.

Narrator: Once again, the prince went to see the master-maid.

Master-Maid: What does the giant expect of you today?

Prince: I have to go underground to collect his taxes. I hope you can tell me what to do. I have never been underground, and I wouldn't even know how much to demand.

Master-Maid: Here is what you must do. Go to the rock under the mountain ridge. Take the club that is there. Knock on the rocky wall. Someone who will sparkle with fire will come out. Tell him your errand. When he asks you how much you want, tell him you want all you can carry.

Narrator: The young people spent the day visiting. Finally, it grew late. The prince left to do exactly as the master-maid had told him. He found the rock and rapped the club on the rocky wall.

Guard: What do you want?

Prince: I came here for the giant. He wants his taxes.

Guard: How much are you asking for?

Prince: I am asking only for what I can carry.

Guard: You are wise. Come in with me.

From *Multicultural Folktales: Readers Theatre for Elementary Students.* © 2000 Suzanne I. Barchers. Teacher Ideas Press. 1-800-237-6124.

Narrator: The prince went in and saw a huge quantity of gold and silver. He collected what he could carry and then returned to the giant's home. Soon the giant came home.

Giant: Have you collected the taxes?

Prince: Yes I have, master.

Giant: Show me.

Prince: The bag of gold is on the bench.

Giant: You have been talking with my master-maid again!

Prince: Master-maid? You keep talking about a master-maid. I wish I could see this for myself!

Giant: Just wait until tomorrow. Then I'll take you to her myself.

Narrator: True to his word, the giant took the prince to the master-maid the next morning.

Giant: Now, master-maid, here is what you must do. Kill the prince and boil him in the cauldron. When the broth is ready, call me.

Narrator: The giant lay down on a bench and fell asleep. The master-maid took a knife and cut the prince's finger a bit. She dripped a few drops of blood on a stool. Then she took all the old rags and rubbish she could find and put them in the cauldron. Next, she filled a chest with gold dust, a lump of salt, and a water flask. She also took away a golden apple and two golden chickens. The young people then ran away as fast as they could. Soon they boarded a ship and sailed away. Finally, the giant woke up.

Giant: Is the cauldron boiling yet?

Drop of Blood: It is just beginning.

Narrator: The giant went back to sleep for another hour or so. Then he woke up.

Giant: Is it ready now?

Drop of Blood: It's half done!

Narrator: The giant slept for a bit more.

Giant: Is it ready yet?

Drop of Blood: It's quite ready.

Narrator: The giant sat up, but he couldn't see who had spoken to him. He called for the master-maid, but there was no answer. He went to the cauldron and realized what had happened. He raced after the young couple, but couldn't cross the sea without a boat. He called for his river-sucker to drink up the water. But the master-maid threw out the lump of salt. It caused a mountain to grow up, stopping the giant and the river-sucker. The giant called for his hill-borer to bore through the mountain, but the master-maid threw out some water from the flask and the sea filled again with water. Soon the prince and master-maid were safe.

Prince: I want to take you to my father, but I don't want you to arrive on foot. Wait here while I go home for the horses.

Master-Maid: Don't leave me! You'll forget me once you reach the palace.

Prince: How could I forget you? We have gone through too much together. I'll be back soon.

Master-Maid: If you must go, at least follow these directions. Go straight to the stable without stopping anywhere else. Collect the coach and horses and drive back as quickly as you can. Act as if you see nothing and be sure not to taste anything. If you do, we will meet with great misery.

Narrator: The prince intended to follow her directions. But when he got to the palace, he learned that his brother was about to be married. All his relatives gathered about, asking him questions. But he pretended not to see anyone and went straight to the stable. But when the bride's sister tossed him an apple, he forgot and took a bite out of it. He immediately forgot the master-maid. Before long, he found he was quite enchanted with the bride's sister and thought he might marry her.

Meanwhile, the master-maid waited for him. Finally, she began to walk and came to a small hut. She asked to stay, not knowing that the owner was an evil troll. The troll let her stay and work for her food and room. The master-maid wanted to spruce up the house, but the troll got angry. The master-maid threw a bit of her gold dust into the fire. The gold dust boiled up and began to cover the whole house with gold. The troll was so terrified, she ran through the door and never returned. Next morning, the sheriff came by and marveled at the golden house. He went inside and was more amazed at seeing such a beautiful young woman.

Sheriff: Good morning, young lady. What an amazing home you have here.

Master-Maid: It is beautiful, isn't it?

Sheriff: You know, I think we should get to know each other better.

Master-Maid: I would like that, but do you have any money?

Sheriff: Oh, yes, I have enough. Perhaps I'll return with it tonight and show you.

Narrator: The sheriff returned that evening with a bag of money. He set it down to show the master-maid. Then he began to talk to her about marriage.

Master-Maid: I'll think about marrying you, but first I must tend the fire.

Sheriff: Let me do that! You just sit right here.

Master-Maid: Just tell me when you have gotten hold of the shovel.

Sheriff: I have hold of it now.

Master-Maid: Then you will hold the shovel tight and shovel until the dawn!

Narrator: Thus, the sheriff was stuck in one spot, shoveling all night. When dawn came, he ran away as fast as he could. He told no one what had happened to him. Next, an attorney came riding by the golden house. He stopped and came in, determined that he would marry the beautiful young woman who lived there.

Master-Maid: Do you have enough money to support a wife?

Attorney: I have ample money. I can care for us very well. I'll go get it and return tonight to show you.

Narrator: That night, the attorney returned with two sacks of money.

Attorney: See, my dear. I have plenty of money for the two of us.

Master-Maid: Yes, that is a lot of money. But now I need to lock the door by the porch.

Attorney: Sit, sit. I'll do that for you.

Master-Maid: Tell me when you have hold of the door latch.

Attorney: I have hold of it now.

Master-Maid: Then you may hold the door and dance between the walls until day dawns!

Narrator: By morning, the attorney was quite exhausted from dancing from wall to wall. As soon as morning came and the door let loose of him, he dashed away. He forgot the young lady and his money in his haste to be away. On the next day, the bailiff came by. He saw the house and the master-maid and decided he had to have both for his own.

Master-Maid: You look fine to me, bailiff. But do you have a lot of money?

Bailiff: I am quite comfortable. Would you like to see? I can bring my money back tonight.

Master-Maid: That would suit me, sir.

Narrator: The bailiff returned with even more money. They sat down, but then the master-maid remembered a chore she needed to do.

Master-Maid: Excuse me, but I have forgotten to bring in the calf.

Bailiff: Oh, no! I can do that for you!

Master-Maid: Tell me when you have got hold of the calf's tail.

Bailiff: I have it now!

Master-Maid: Then you will hold the calf's tail and go around the world together until dawn!

Narrator: The bailiff could do nothing but follow the calf as it walked over hill and dale. When daylight came, the bailiff was half dead. He was so glad to be loose that he forgot his plans to marry and left behind his sack of money.

The next day was the wedding at the palace. The elder brother and his bride joined the prince and the bride's sister in a coach. But one of the pins on the coach broke and no matter how hard everyone tried, the coach would not be repaired. The sheriff, who was invited to the wedding, saw their trouble.

Sheriff: If you want a strong piece of wood, go to the little house in the woods. Ask for the handle of the shovel. I know it will hold fast.

Narrator: The members of the wedding party sent a messenger for the shovel handle, which the master-maid readily gave. They repaired the coach, but then the bottom fell out. They kept trying to fix it, but it only broke apart again. The attorney, who was also at the wedding, had an idea.

Attorney: Go to the little house in the woods. Ask the woman if you could have the door. I know it won't break.

Narrator: The members of the wedding party sent the messenger back and he borrowed the door. Soon the coach was fixed and they set out again. This time, the horses could not pull the coach. They added two, four, and six. But still the coach would not budge. The bailiff spoke up this time.

Bailiff: Go to the little house in the woods. Ask for the loan of the lady's calf. I know it could pull the coach anywhere!

Narrator: The members of the wedding party thought having a calf pull a coach was foolish, but they had no choice. They borrowed the calf and harnessed it. Away it went, moving so fast that they sped to the church in a flash. Their return to the palace for the wedding party was equally speedy. The prince decided they should invite to the party the young woman who had helped them so much. The king sent his messengers to ask if the young woman would come to the wedding party.

Master-Maid: Tell the king that if he wants me to come, he should ask me himself.

Narrator: So the king fetched the master-maid himself. He seated her at the head table in honor of her help. She took out the golden chickens and the golden apple, which she had brought from the giant's house. The chickens began to fight over the golden apple.

Prince: Look how those chickens are fighting over the golden apple!

Master-Maid: Yes, and so did we fight to get out of the giant's house!

Narrator: With that the prince remembered that the master-maid was his true love. He announced that this was the woman he would marry. Everyone celebrated his brother's wedding, and they looked forward happily to the next wedding.

The Tree That Bled Fish

Micronesia

Summary

Kodep's job is to gather fish from a special tree that bleeds seawater and fish. But when he begins to chop too many branches, he is warned to let the tree rest for a year. Thinking that evil spirits are at work, the villagers chop down most of the tree. But Kodep heeds the warning that if left alone, the tree will replenish and provide them with breadfruit. They wait a year and then enjoy the special fruit from the tree.

Presentation Suggestions

Kodep and the narrator have primary roles and can stand on one side of the stage. The old woman can be on the opposite side, with the children and villagers between them.

Props

If possible, decorate the stage with a South Pacific motif. Students can create a mural with typical patterns of the cloth worn by islanders. The students can wear simple clothing. Try to obtain breadfruit, placing it on the stage.

Delivery Suggestions

The old woman should sound sorrowful and persistent. Kodep should sound wary of her voice at first, but then convinced. The children, man, and woman should sound disbelieving. The chief should sound powerful.

Characters

Narrator
Kodep
Old Woman
First Child
Second Child
Man
Woman
Chief

"The Tree That Bled Fish" was adapted from "The Tree That Bled Fish" in *From the Mouth of the Monster Eel: Stories from Micronesia* by Bo Flood, illustrated by Margo Vitarelli (Golden, CO: Fulcrum, 1996), 25–31. Used with permission.

The Tree That Bled Fish

Narrator: Kodep licked his fingers, smacked his lips, and rubbed his full stomach. He looked up at the tree that had fed him his favorite food, fish. He would not need to chop off another branch until evening. He decided to rest. As he began to sleep, a sad moaning drifted into his dream. He seemed to hear cries from an old woman. He woke up and looked around.

Kodep: I must have eaten too much fish!

Narrator: Kodep closed his eyes again. Then he heard the sad moaning again.

Old Woman: Kodep! Remember the warning, Kodep!

Kodep: Whoever you are, go away!

Old Woman: Kodep! Remember the warning, Kodep!

Kodep: Whoever you are, tell me why you are trying to scare me!

Narrator: Kodep remembered the story his father had told him about a strange tree that bled fish. Long ago, when the village was starving, this tall, giant tree appeared. The message the people heard instructed them to take care of the tree. Then the tree would take care of them. If they took too much, there would be nothing. At first the villagers were afraid of the tree. But one day, when a branch broke off, seawater filled with fish streamed out. People began to come to the tree for fish. It was Kodep's job to cut off a branch every day and catch the fish that poured forth.

Kodep: If I can't rest, then I will work.

Narrator: Kodep climbed on a branch and began to chop. The branch beneath his feet snapped. He crashed to the ground and landed in a puddle of seawater, fish, and mud.

Old Woman: Do not cut another limb. This tree was given to all so that children could survive drought and typhoon. Let the tree blossom and its fruit will feed you.

Narrator: Kodep looked around him, but could see no one. He grabbed his basket and ran back to the village. He told the people about the voice. The children laughed at his story.

First Child: Kodep, you are trying to trick us.

Second Child: You ate too many fish. Now you are afraid of your own bad dreams!

Narrator: The old men and women didn't laugh. They looked at the lagoon where no one had fished for months. They looked at those making fun of Kodep. They walked silently to their huts. They ate their evening meal in silence and then tried to sleep. The next day, Kodep took some friends to the tree.

Kodep: Help me gather fish. Today we will cut many branches and fill every basket. Tonight we will heap wood onto a leaping fire, eat until we are bursting, and dance until we sleep.

Narrator: They gathered around the tree and began to cut the bark. They heard a soft moan.

Kodep: This is foolishness. A tree is just a tree. It is meant to be cut, to bleed, to die.

Old Woman: Do not cut this tree. This breadfruit tree was given to all generations. Do not kill it branch by branch. Protect its life and this tree will nourish you with bread.

First Child: This is a trick.

Second Child: An evil spirit has bewitched this place.

First Child: Cut down the tree. That will stop it.

Second Child: Let's destroy the evil spirits before they destroy us!

Kodep: But someone keeps calling me. I don't understand, but I must find out who it is.

Narrator: Kodep began walking away from the village. He walked to a hut tucked under the jagged rocks of a lava cliff. He found an old woman waiting inside.

Old Woman: I cry for the tree. This tree will nourish you with its fruit. It is the only tree of its kind and you are destroying it branch by branch. If it dies, you will have nothing. If it lives, it will provide food.

Kodep: But the tree gives us fish. I am satisfied with fish.

Old Woman: But you are not thinking beyond today. Fish swarm in the lagoon. Hunt wisely, let the fish replenish themselves, and you will always have fish. Care for this tree. Do not kill it. Act wisely and you will always have the breadfruit that will grow on it.

Kodep: But if I return without food, the people will be angry and throw stones.

Narrator: The woman said nothing.

Kodep: If I tell them your words, they will laugh and call me a fool. Why should they hunt fish in the lagoon when fish bleed from this tree? They will never believe your words.

Narrator: The woman said nothing. Kodep thought about the breadfruit tree he had often climbed. Many branches remained, but many were gone. He returned to the village. The people gathered around and asked many questions.

Man: Where were you, Kodep? Napping again?

Woman: Where is our supper?

Man: Our stomachs are rumbling.

Woman: Where are the baskets of fish?

Kodep: It's time to hunt in the lagoon and let the tree rest and its fruit ripen.

Man: You have been dreaming.

Woman: This tree has never grown fruit. You are just lazy, making excuses so you don't have to work.

Kodep: But the woman said that we will kill the tree unless we let it rest.

Man: Go back to the tree. Your job is to gather fish from it. Go!

Narrator: Just then, the chief stepped forward.

Chief: Wait! Perhaps there is some truth to what Kodep says. We will wait one year. The tree will rest and we will watch for this fruit called breadfruit. After a year, if there is no breadfruit, we will begin chopping.

Narrator: Many months passed before blossoms appeared in the highest limbs. More months crept by before bumpy green fruit was seen hanging from thin stalks. Slowly, the fruit grew and grew, becoming round and heavy. The chief called for Kodep.

Chief: It is time to cut the tree. Bring me the fruit.

Narrator: Kodep climbed the tree and cut off large green fruit, the breadfruit. He placed it on the fire and roasted it with the reef fish on top of steaming banana leaves. He gave the breadfruit to the chief to taste. The chief nodded for Kodep to taste it first. He peeled off the outer skin and popped a piece of the hot yellow fruit into his mouth. Everyone watched while Kodep chewed.

Kodep smiled. He ate another piece, and then another. He rubbed his stomach. Everyone began nibbling the chunks of roasted breadfruit. Soon they all rubbed their full, full stomachs. And from that time forward, even during times of famine, drought, or typhoon, breadfruit trees on the islands of the Pacific are honored and protected. Roasted breadfruit fills hungry stomachs and children whisper, "Thank you, breadfruit tree."

Water, Water Will Be Mine

Kenya

Summary

When the water dries up, all the animals, except for Sungura the Rabbit, work together to dig a new water hole. Rabbit isn't allowed to drink because he hasn't helped. But he repeatedly tricks the guards into letting him drink. Finally, the animals set a trap, and Kaa the Crab catches him in the act. The animals plan to punish him, but once again he outsmarts them and gets away.

Presentation Suggestions

There are many characters in this story, but the ones with the most lines include the narrator, Simba the Lion, Sungura the Rabbit, Tumbili the Monkey, and Tumbili the Monkey's Brother. These characters should have prominent positions. Mamba the Crocodile, Chui the Leopard, Kuro the Waterbuck, Ngiri the Warthog, Chura Kodgo, Chura Katikati, Chura Kikubwa, and Kaa the Crab may sit down after their lines.

Props

A mural that resembles an African water hole could serve as a backdrop. Because there are so many characters, it would be helpful to the audience for each character to wear a sign displaying his or her name. Sungura the Rabbit could wear a frayed rope around his waist.

Delivery Suggestions

Simba the Lion should sound bold and authoritative. Sungura the Rabbit should sound persuasive and clever. The monkeys should sound rather gullible. The other animals can use voices appropriate to their roles.

Characters

Narrator
Simba the Lion
Mamba the Crocodile
Chui the Leopard
Kuro the Waterbuck
Ngiri the Warthog
Sungura the Rabbit

Chura Kodgo
Chura Katikati
Chura Kikubwa
Tumbili the Monkey
Tumbili the Monkey's Brother
Kaa the Crab

"Water, Water Will Be Mine" was adapted from "Water, Water Will Be Mine" in *Hyena and the Moon: Stories to Tell from Kenya* by Heather McNeil (Englewood, CO: Libraries Unlimited, 1994), 86–94. Used with permission.

Water, Water Will Be Mine

Narrator: Long ago there was a time of no rain. The rivers, lakes, mud holes, and rock holes were all dry. The animals had nothing to drink and knew they would die soon. So it was that they all came together to talk about water.

Simba the Lion: Who can find us water? Mamba, we must have water. Where is the water you swim in every day?

Mamba the Crocodile: There is no water. I do not swim anymore. Instead I crawl on the earth, just like Mjusi the Lizard.

Simba the Lion: But we must have water. Chui, where is the water you drink every day?

Chui the Leopard: There is no water. I do not drink anymore. I eat dust, like Muhanga the Aardvark in the termite hill.

Simba the Lion: Kuro, we must have water. Where is the water that is always beside your feet?

Kuro the Waterbuck: There is no water. There is only dust under my feet, as it is under all of our feet.

Narrator: Lion asked the other animals, and to everyone's surprise, it was Ngiri the Warthog who had an answer.

Ngiri the Warthog: The water is in the ground.

Simba the Lion: Where did you say the water is?

Ngiri the Warthog: It is in the ground.

Simba the Lion: Where in the ground?

Ngiri the Warthog: It is deep in the ground. Sometimes I can smell it in my hole. But I cannot dig deep enough to find it.

Simba the Lion: Then we must all dig, deep into the earth. And then everyone will share in the water that we find.

Narrator: Everyone agreed to help except for Sungura the Rabbit, who was very lazy.

Sungura the Rabbit: You go ahead and dig while I watch.

Simba the Lion: If you don't dig, you will not drink.

Narrator: But Sungura just laughed. The animals began to dig. With paws and claws and tusks and teeth, they dug and they dug and they dug. It was Chura Kodgo, the small frog, who saw the first trickle of water and began to sing.

Chura Kodgo: Water sweet, water fine.
Water, water will be mine.
Be-deep! Be-deep! Be-deep!

Narrator: Chura Katikati, the middle-sized frog, sang as the water began to fill the hole.

Chura Katikati: Water sweet, water fine.
Water, water will be mine.
Go-deep! Go-deep! Go-deep!

Narrator: Finally, Chura Kikubwa, the giant frog, sang, too.

Chura Kikubwa: Water sweet, water fine.
Water, water will be mine.
Now-deep! Now-deep! Now-deep!

Narrator: The animals began to drink—slurping, lapping, and licking. The lazy rabbit watched.

Simba the Lion: Sungura, you did not dig, so you shall not drink.

Sungura the Rabbit: Ha, I'm not worried!

Narrator: The next morning when the animals returned to the water hole, they found fresh footprints in the mud. They knew whom the footprints belonged to. The lion called a meeting.

Simba the Lion: We agreed that all the animals would dig and all the animals would drink. But Sungura did not dig and therefore Sungura will not drink! Tumbili, I am assigning you to guard the water hole.

Narrator: That day, Tumbili the Monkey waited. He looked up, down, and all around. He wiggled and squirmed and finally decided to hide in the grass. Just as the sun was about to set, Sungura, that lazy rabbit, came down the road. He carried a gourd in one hand and a stick in the other.

Sungura the Rabbit: Water sweet, water fine.
Water, water will be mine.

Narrator: Sungura hit the water with his stick. Tumbili the Monkey popped out of the grass.

Sungura the Rabbit: Hello, Tumbili, how are you this fine, fine evening?

Tumbili the Monkey: Go away, Rabbit. You aren't drinking any of this water.

Sungura the Rabbit: Why would I want any of that dirty water, Tumbili, when I have all of this sweet, sweet water?

Tumbili the Monkey: What sweet, sweet water?

Sungura the Rabbit: The water in this gourd. Why, it is sweet as honey.

Tumbili the Monkey: As sweet as honey?

Sungura the Rabbit: Yes, Tumbili, as sweet as honey.

Tumbili the Monkey: Where did you get that water? This hole has all the water there is.

Sungura the Rabbit: No, that is not all the water.

Tumbili the Monkey: Let me taste your water and see if it is really as sweet as honey.

Narrator: Rabbit poured the sweet, thick, golden liquid into Tumbili the Monkey's mouth. Monkey drank every last drop.

Sungura the Rabbit: Tumbili, you drank all my water! Now what will I drink?

Tumbili the Monkey: I'm sorry, Sungura. Please drink the water in the hole. Drink all you want.

Narrator: And the lazy, lazy rabbit did just that. In the morning, Simba the Lion roared with anger.

Simba the Lion: Tumbili, why is more water gone?

Tumbili the Monkey: Well, Sungura came with a gourd full of water as sweet as honey. He let me taste it, and I drank it all. I had to let him drink our water.

Simba the Lion: I will have to have another monkey guard the hole. Your brother should do quite well.

Narrator: That night, Tumbili the Monkey's Brother hid in the grass. Soon the lazy rabbit came down the road, swinging a stick in one hand and a gourd in the other.

Sungura the Rabbit: Water sweet, water fine,
Water, water will be mine.

Narrator: Sungura hit the water with his stick. Tumbili the Monkey's Brother popped out of the grass.

Sungura the Rabbit: Hello Tumbili, how are you this fine, fine evening?

Tumbili the Monkey's Brother: Go away, Sungura. I know about you and how you tricked my brother.

Sungura the Rabbit: I did not trick your brother. I just gave him some of my sweet, sweet water.

Tumbili the Monkey's Brother: What sweet water? The only water is in this hole.

Sungura the Rabbit: No, Monkey. I have my own sweet water. Why, it's as sweet as honey.

Tumbili the Monkey's Brother: As sweet as honey?

Sungura the Rabbit: Would you like to taste it?

Narrator: Sungura poured the thick, sweet, golden liquid into Tumbili the Monkey's Brother's mouth. Tumbili the Monkey's Brother drank every last drop.

Sungura the Rabbit: Monkey, you drank all my water! Now what will I drink?

Tumbili the Monkey's Brother: I am so sorry, Sungura. Please drink the water in the hole. Drink all you want.

Narrator: And the lazy, lazy rabbit did. The next morning, Simba chose another monkey to guard the water, but the same thing happened. And the next morning, it happened again. And the next morning. Soon there were no more monkeys left.

Simba the Lion: Who will catch Sungura?

Narrator: No one answered. Simba asked each of the animals in turn, but none knew what to do. Finally, he came to Kaa the Crab.

Simba the Lion: Kaa, you will catch Sungura!

Kaa the Crab: Me? But I am only a crab!

Simba the Lion: Yes, you are a crab. And where do crabs live?

Kaa the Crab: In sand, on rocks, in the water.

Simba the Lion: Yes, Kaa, in the water. And what does the claw of a crab do?

Kaa the Crab: Pinch, scratch, catch!

Simba the Lion: Yes, Kaa, they catch. Will you help us?

Kaa the Crab: I will try.

Narrator: Kaa scuttled down into the hole and disappeared into the water. Just as the sun was ready to sleep, down the road came that lazy, lazy rabbit, gourd in one hand and a stick in the other. Just as before, he sang as he walked.

Sungura the Rabbit: Water sweet, water fine,
        Water, water will be mine.

Narrator: Sungura hit the water with his stick. Nothing happened. He hit the water with his stick again. Still nothing.

Sungura the Rabbit: No one is guarding the hole. So I will drink.

Narrator: Sungura leaned over the hole. He put out his two front paws and filled them with cool, sweet water. He closed his eyes, bent his head down and then—SWSSHH! SNAP! CLICK! Crab's huge claw clamped around Rabbit's paws and held him tight. It was a long night for Sungura. He begged and pleaded. He tried to shake off Kaa. He tried to trick Kaa into drinking some of his thick, golden liquid. But Kaa just held on tighter and did not listen. In the morning, the animals found Sungura sitting quietly.

Simba the Lion: So, Kaa. You are not just a crab! Today you are a hero! You have caught the lazy, lazy rabbit. Now we shall end his days!

Sungura the Rabbit: Yes, it is best that I end my days here at the water hole.

Simba the Lion: I'm glad you agree, Sungura. Now, how shall we end your days? What do you fear the most?

Sungura the Rabbit: Flying.

Simba the Lion: Flying? But you cannot fly, Sungura.

Sungura the Rabbit: Exactly. So, please don't throw me up in the air. Elephant, you can trample me. Python, you can squeeze me. Crocodile, you can swallow me. Just please, please, please, do not throw me up into the air!

Simba the Lion: Of course, we will not. But if we did throw you into the air, just exactly how would we do it?

Sungura the Rabbit: You would tie all my paws together with the rope from around my waist. Elephant would swing me around and around, throw me up into the air, and I would come down, dead.

Simba the Lion: Dead?

Sungura the Rabbit: Dead. Flat, like the grass beneath your feet.

Simba the Lion: That is a terrible thing, a terrible way to end your days at the water hole. So that is exactly what we will do!

Narrator: Simba untied the old, frayed rope from around Sungura the Rabbit's middle and tied all four of his paws together. Only then did he tell Kaa to let go. Lion called for Tembo the Elephant. Tembo took the end of the rope in his trunk. He raised it high in the air, lifting Rabbit off the ground. He began to swing Rabbit around and around and around.

Sungura the Rabbit: Oh please, Tembo. Not so fast.

Simba the Lion: Faster, Tembo, faster!

Sungura the Rabbit: Oh Tembo, please stop!

Narrator: Tembo swung Rabbit around and around and around. Then, SNAP! The rope broke. Rabbit's paws flew out free, and when he fell to the ground, he landed flat on all four of his feet, running. And as he ran, he sang:

Sungura the Rabbit: Water sweet, water fine,
Water, water will be mine!

The White-Haired Old Woman

United States, Native American

Summary

When an old woman and her grandson are sent away from their tribe, they search for a tribe to take pity on them. Finally, a poor tribe takes them in. The old woman offers to care for the children, who enjoy her stories. She also provides a midday meal of maize gruel for the children. Before she dies, she plants the maize grain so that the tribe never goes hungry again.

Presentation Suggestions

This is a short play. All the characters can be placed in prominent positions on the stage.

Props

This is a good script for the fall season. Decorate the stage with cornstalks, squash, and gourds. If possible, have corn that shows the silk. A pot can be placed on the stage for the maize gruel. Students can research appropriate harvest symbols for a mural.

Delivery Suggestions

The grandson can sound tired at the beginning of the script. The old woman should sound weary, but very wise and patient. The chief should sound regal.

Characters

Narrator
Grandson
Old Woman
Chief

From *Multicultural Folktales: Readers Theatre for Elementary Students.* © 2000 Suzanne I. Barchers. Teacher Ideas Press. 1-800-237-6124.

The White-Haired Old Woman

Narrator: Once there was an old, white-haired woman. She and her grandson were sent away from their tribe. They traveled for a long time, looking for a tribe that would take them in. Again and again they were turned away.

Grandson: Grandmother, I am hungry and tired. When can we stop?

Old Woman: We can't stop now. We have to keep looking for help.

Narrator: Finally, they came to a tribe that took pity on them.

Chief: We have little here. Our hunters try to find game, but we often go hungry. However, you are welcome to share what we have.

Old Woman: Thank you for your kindness. I would like to help here. I can take care of the children while their mothers work.

Chief: We welcome your help. The children will surely learn from your wisdom.

Narrator: One day, all the adults left to hunt and gather food. The children were content to play. The old woman told many stories, and the children found that the hours passed quickly. They were also happy to have a meal at midday. Each day, the old woman left for a while. When she returned, she would bring a kettle of gruel.

Old Woman: Children, this is maize gruel. If you behave, I will feed you every day.

Narrator: The children never gave the old woman a minute's trouble. Each day, they played happily. Each day, the old woman brought the children their gruel. They were grateful to have a midday meal. Many years passed. The old woman began to feel her age. She grew tired and frail. One morning, she called her grandson to her.

Grandson: What is it, Grandmother? Do you need something?

Old Woman: My time to leave you grows near. But I am content. I have finished my job here. I have planted the maize grains near the camp. They have taken root. All that is left is for you and the children to water and tend them. The grain will sprout in the spring. With love and care, you will have a harvest in the fall.

Grandson: I will see that the maize grows strong, Grandmother.

Narrator: The old woman never spoke again. She stayed in her bed, living through summer until harvest came. But each noon there was a kettle of maize gruel for the children. Finally, the old woman disappeared forever. The chief called the tribe together.

Chief: The old woman has repaid us many times over. We will never again be hungry if we tend the maize with the same love she showed us.

Narrator: The old woman's love is remembered every year when the corn shows its white hairs.

From *Multicultural Folktales: Readers Theatre for Elementary Students.* © 2000 Suzanne I. Barchers. Teacher Ideas Press. 1-800-237-6124.

Why Ants Carry Burdens

Africa/Hausa

Summary

Anansi's farm and his son's farms are both suffering from lack of rain. When Anansi's son gets help from a little man, rain falls on his farm. Anansi decides to get help from the same man, but he kills the man instead. Anansi tries to make his son take the blame for the little man's death, knowing that the man was the king's favorite jester. Instead, Anansi's son tricks Anansi into taking the little man's body to the king, who makes Anansi carry the body in a box until he can convince someone else to carry it. Finally, Anansi convinces Ant to carry it, sentencing ants to always carry burdens.

Presentation Suggestions

The narrator should stand to one side. The little man should stand between Anansi and his son, with Ant on the other side.

Props

The characters can be dressed in clothing with earth tones to represent Africa. The stage can have a mural with a farm as a backdrop. Farming implements could decorate the stage.

Delivery Suggestions

The little man could have a small, high voice. Anansi should sound smooth and convincing, especially when he is convincing Ant to take on the box. Anansi's son should use a normal voice.

Characters

Narrator
Little Man
Son
Anansi
King
Ant

Why Ants Carry Burdens

Narrator: Anansi and his son were both clever farmers. They each had their own farm and usually had fine harvests. But one year little rain fell, and it looked as though their seeds would never sprout. One day, Anansi's son was walking along, feeling very sad, when he met a little man by the road.

Little Man: Why are you so sad?

Son: No rain has come for many weeks, and my seeds are not sprouting. My life will be miserable if my crops fail.

Little Man: I think I can help you. Fetch two small sticks. Then tap me lightly on my back and sing these words:
> Water go up. Water go up.
> Let the rain fall. Let the rain fall.

Narrator: It immediately began to rain steadily on the son's farm, and the ground soaked up all the rain hungrily. In a short time, the seeds sprouted, ensuring a good crop after all. But it didn't rain on Anansi's farm, and when Anansi noticed his son's successful crop, he went to see him.

Anansi: Tell me, son, how is it that you have such a wonderful crop?

Son: Father, I met a little man who offered to help me. All I had to do was take two little sticks and tap on his back while saying a little chant. Then the rains came and soaked the dry ground.

Narrator: Anansi decided that he had to find this little man and get rain for his crops, too. On the way, he talked to himself.

Anansi: If my son got rain with little sticks, I will use big sticks and get even more from the little man.

Narrator: Soon he saw the little man, and realized that he was the king's favorite jester. The little man greeted Anansi in the same way that he had greeted Anansi's son.

Little Man: Why are you so sad?

Anansi: My farm is dry with no rain. If no rain falls, my seeds won't sprout, and I will starve.

Little Man: I think I can help you. Fetch two small sticks. Then tap me lightly on my back and sing these words:
> Water go up. Water go up.
> Let the rain fall. Let the rain fall.

From *Multicultural Folktales: Readers Theatre for Elementary Students.* © 2000 Suzanne I. Barchers. Teacher Ideas Press. 1-800-237-6124.

Narrator: But Anansi took two big sticks and hit the little man so hard that he killed him. He was horrified at what he had done, knowing that the king would be very angry. He decided to hide the little man's body in the branches of a tree. Then he sat down under the tree as if nothing had happened. Soon Anansi's son came by to see if Anansi had succeeded in getting rain for his farm.

Son: Hello, Father. Did you meet the little man?

Anansi: Oh yes, but he climbed this tree and hasn't come back down. I've been waiting for him.

Son: Maybe something is wrong. I'll go up and fetch him.

Narrator: But when Anansi's son climbed the tree, the little man's body fell out and landed hard on the ground.

Anansi: Oh no, you wicked boy, you have killed the king's jester!

Narrator: The son realized that his father was trying to trick him into taking the blame for the jester's death.

Son: That is all right, Father. I recently heard that the jester has fallen into disfavor with the king. The king promised a bag of money to anyone who would kill him, so I will just take his body and collect the reward.

Anansi: No, no! I killed him with two big sticks, so I deserve the reward. I will take him to the king.

Son: Well, I see that you are truly the one who deserves the reward, so take him away.

Narrator: Anansi proudly carried the jester's body to the king's court.

Anansi: Your Majesty, I have brought you the body of the jester, whom I recently killed.

King: How could you kill my favorite jester and then present him to me like this? You shall be punished! I am going to put the jester in a box. Now this isn't just any box. It is an enchanted box, and you will be required to carry it with you for the rest of your days. The only way you can be rid of it is to convince someone else to carry it for you.

Narrator: Anansi was appalled by his sentence, but knew that he had little choice in the matter. He knew that no one would take over the carrying of the box, so he put it on his head as ordered. One day, when Anansi was nearly dead from exhaustion, he met Ant.

Anansi: Ant, will you hold this box for me while I tend my crops?

Ant: Do you think I am a fool? I know you are just trying to trick me to get rid of your burden.

Anansi: Truly, I will come back for it. If I don't take care of my crops, I will starve this winter.

Ant: All right, but be sure to come back for it straight away.

Narrator: Of course Anansi had no intention of coming back for the box. Ant waited and waited, but realized that he was destined to always carry the box on his head. And that is why ants to this very day often carry burdens on their heads.

From *Multicultural Folktales: Readers Theatre for Elementary Students.* © 2000 Suzanne I. Barchers. Teacher Ideas Press. 1-800-237-6124.

Chapter 4

Fourth-Grade Reading Level

Arion and His Harp

Greece

Summary

When Arion decides to go to Sicily to compete in a music contest, his friend Periander asks him not to go but to remain at his court, where Arion lives. Arion insists on going and wins the contest. On his return, some murdering pirates force Arion overboard so they can steal his treasure. On hearing his last song, a dolphin swims forward to help Arion to shore. When the ship arrives in Corinth, the pirates are caught and sent away.

Presentation Suggestions

The narrator can be placed on the side with Periander next to him. Arion can be in the middle with the pirates on the other side.

Props

Periander can be dressed to look like royalty. Arion can dress like a minstrel, perhaps holding an instrument. The pirates can be dressed with bright sashes, perhaps with seamen's caps. A mural depicting the ocean and islands could be placed in the background.

Delivery Suggestions

Periander should have an authoritative voice. The pirates should sound evil. Arion should have a pleasant, musical voice.

Characters

Narrator
Arion
Periander
First Pirate
Second Pirate

"Arion and His Harp" was adapted from "Arion and His Harp" in *Troubadour's Storybag: Musical Folktales of the World*, retold and edited by Norma J. Livo (Golden, CO: Fulcrum, 1996), 95–97. Used with permission.

Arion and His Harp

Narrator: Arion dwelt in the court of Periander, the king of Corinth. He was the greatest singer of tales and a favorite of Periander. One day, he spoke to Periander about a contest.

Arion: There is going to be a musical contest in Sicily. I want to compete for the prize.

Periander: Why do you need to compete in a contest? Stay with me. Be content here. After all, you may lose.

Arion: But I enjoy wandering. I want to share my talents with others. And I seek the fame that winning will bring me.

Periander: Go then, my friend. But I will miss you and wish you would stay.

Narrator: Arion went to Sicily, where he easily won the contest. He left Sicily for Corinth on a ship carrying a chest full of his reward. He was eager to share his riches with Periander. As Arion strolled on deck, he overheard the seamen plotting to kill him for his riches. He had no way to escape when the crew came for him.

First Pirate: Arion, you must die! If you want to be buried onshore, surrender to us. Otherwise, throw yourself into the sea.

Arion: Take my gold if that is what you want. But spare my life.

Second Pirate: No! You must die. If you live, you would tell Periander and we would be punished.

Arion: Before I die, please grant me one last wish. I would like to die as I have lived, as a bard singing and playing my harp. Then I will bid farewell to life and go to my fate.

First Pirate: So you want to sing for us? Well, we do like music.

Second Pirate: I think we can grant that wish. A last song seems little enough to grant.

Arion: If it pleases you, I would like to dress in proper clothes for such an important performance. Apollo would be disappointed to meet me unless I was dressed in my minstrel garments.

First Pirate: You are testing me, but I see nothing wrong with your request.

Narrator: Arion dressed himself in his gold and purple tunic. He put jewels on his arms and a golden wreath on his head. He held his lyre in his left hand and struck it with an ivory wand. He appeared to be inspired as he gazed on the glittering morning sunlight. He began to sing of his new life among the gods and wise ones. As he finished, he turned and leapt off the boat. He soon disappeared from sight under the waves. The crew felt safe and continued to Corinth. The crew didn't know that the song had charmed the sea creatures. A dolphin swam up and offered to carry Arion safely to shore. Arion returned to Periander's court and told him what had happened. When the ship arrived in the harbor, Periander summoned the crew before him.

Periander: Have you had a good trip?

First Pirate: Yes, Your Majesty. It was a fine trip.

Periander: Did you by chance hear anything about my friend Arion? I am quite anxious for his return.

Second Pirate: We did see him. But we left him well and prosperous in Tarentum.

Narrator: Just then, Arion stepped forward and faced them.

Arion: So you left me in Tarentum, you say?

First Pirate: We thought you were dead!

Second Pirate: Have you returned as a god?

Periander: Arion isn't a god. He lives as a man, the master of music. You greedy murderers are lucky that he doesn't seek his revenge. Be gone with you all. May your lives never experience the sights and sounds of beauty again.

Narrator: Arion had many more years left to him. He created wonderful music and sang the praises of the dolphins.

Catherine and Her Destiny

Italy, Sicily

Summary

Catherine has to choose between happiness in her youth or in her old age. She chooses happiness in her old age and faces many challenges for the rest of her youth. Finally, she meets a lady who helps her turn her destiny to good fortune. Thanks to a ball of beautiful silk, she meets the king who chooses her for his wife.

Presentation Suggestions

Because the merchant has only a few lines, he should leave the stage or sit down after his part. The first lady and second lady could also leave the stage or sit down after their lines. The narrator, Destiny, and Catherine have central roles.

Props

Catherine can be dressed simply. The three ladies can be dressed in elegant clothes. The characters of Destiny can also be dressed in beautiful clothes. A wheel can be propped on the stage to symbolize the wheel of destiny.

Delivery Suggestions

The merchant should sound sad and resigned. Catherine should sound humble and determined to survive her destiny. The ladies should sound sympathetic and helpful. The king should sound powerful and regal.

Characters

Narrator
Destiny
Catherine
Merchant
First Lady
Second Lady
Third Lady
Third Lady's Destiny
King

Catherine and Her Destiny

Narrator: Long ago, a rich merchant possessed more treasures than any king in the world. But his greatest treasure of all was his daughter, Catherine. One day, Catherine was sitting in her room when a tall, beautiful woman entered. The woman held a little wheel in her hands.

Destiny: Catherine, which would you rather have—a happy youth or a happy old age?

Catherine: Let me think a minute. If I say a happy youth, then I shall have to suffer all the rest of my life. Youth passes quickly. I would rather bear trouble now and have something better to look forward to. Give me a happy old age.

Destiny: As you wish.

Narrator: The lady, who was Catherine's Destiny, disappeared. Only a few days later, the merchant called Catherine to him.

Merchant: Catherine, I have received grave news. All my ships were sunk in a storm. I have nothing left.

Catherine: Father, don't worry. I know we can find a way to live comfortably.

Merchant: My dear, I am not sure what we will do. Right now I feel poorly.

Narrator: The merchant took to his bed, and before long he died from a broken heart. Catherine decided her only course of action was to go to the nearest town and seek work as a servant. As she walked through the town, a noble lady saw her and was struck by her sad face.

First Lady: Where are you going all alone, my pretty girl?

Catherine: Ah, my lady, I am very poor, and must find work.

First Lady: You can work for me, my dear.

Narrator: Catherine served the lady well, but some time later the lady had to leave for a long time.

First Lady: Catherine, I must be away for a long while. I will have to lock the house door so that no thieves will enter. You must take care in my absence.

Narrator: Catherine kept working at her chores. As she was sitting by the window, Destiny suddenly burst through the door.

Destiny: So here you are, Catherine. Did you really think I was going to leave you in peace? Watch this!

From *Multicultural Folktales: Readers Theatre for Elementary Students.* © 2000 Suzanne I. Barchers. Teacher Ideas Press. 1-800-237-6124.

Narrator: Destiny went to the linen press, where the lady kept her finest sheets, and tore everything into pieces. Catherine began to weep, knowing that her lady would blame her. She ran out through the open door. Then Destiny took all the pieces and made them whole again, putting them neatly away. When the lady returned home, she found the door open and Catherine gone.

First Lady: Can Catherine have robbed me? This is strange. The house is standing wide open, but nothing seems to be missing except for Catherine. Whatever could have happened to her?

Narrator: When Catherine didn't return, the lady hired a new servant. Meanwhile, Catherine wandered on and on, not knowing where she was going. She came to another town, and just as before, a noble lady noticed her passing by.

Second Lady: Where are you going, young girl?

Catherine: My lady, I am very poor and hungry. I must go into service to earn my food.

Second Lady: I will hire you, my dear. Come in and I'll show you what to do.

Narrator: Just as before, Catherine served her well, but she wondered when Destiny would come. One day when Catherine was alone in the house, Destiny appeared.

Destiny: How did you manage to find work, Catherine? I will put an end to that!

Narrator: And just as before, Destiny began to destroy the lady's belongings. Catherine fled from the house, and Destiny restored everything to normal. And so it went for seven years. Each time Catherine found new work, and Destiny arrived and forced Catherine to flee. Finally, Catherine went to work for a third lady, who gave Catherine an unusual task.

Third Lady: Catherine, each day I want you to climb to the top of the mountain, taking these loaves of bread along. When you get to the top, lay the bread on the ground. Repeat the following three times: "O Destiny, my mistress." That will serve as my offering to my Destiny.

Catherine: I will gladly do that, my lady.

Narrator: For years, Catherine climbed the mountain with her basket of bread. She was somewhat content, but sometimes she would be overcome with weeping when thinking about her past life. One day, her lady saw her crying.

Third Lady: Why do you weep? Whatever is the matter, dear?

Narrator: Catherine told her how her destiny had promised to make her youth miserable.

From *Multicultural Folktales: Readers Theatre for Elementary Students.* © 2000 Suzanne I. Barchers. Teacher Ideas Press. 1-800-237-6124.

Third Lady: I have an idea. Tomorrow, when you take the bread to the mountain, pray for my destiny to speak to your destiny. Beg her to leave you in peace. Perhaps that will help.

Narrator: The next morning, Catherine climbed the mountain and told her lady's destiny her story. She begged Destiny to help her. She was startled to hear a voice.

Third Lady's Destiny: My poor dear. Don't you know that your destiny lies buried under seven covers and can hear nothing? Return as usual tomorrow and I will try to bring her with me.

Narrator: As it happened, Catherine's destiny and her lady's destiny were sisters. Her lady's Destiny went to find her sister.

Third Lady's Destiny: Sister, hasn't Catherine suffered enough? Isn't it time for her good days to begin?

Destiny: Bring her to me tomorrow. I will give her something that will help her.

Narrator: The next morning, Catherine arrived as promised and was led to Destiny, who lay buried under her seven covers.

Destiny: Catherine, I am giving you this ball of silk. Keep it always. It may be useful one day.

Narrator: Catherine sadly took the ball of silk to the lady.

Catherine: What shall I do with this? It is hardly worth anything.

Third Lady: Keep it, my dear. You never know when it might be useful.

Narrator: A short time later, grand preparations were under way for the king's marriage. All the tailors were embroidering fine clothes. The wedding clothes were almost finished when the tailor found he had no more silk. The color was unusual, and no one could find more. The king proclaimed that anyone who had some matching silk would receive a rich reward. The lady saw the clothes and realized that Catherine's silk was exactly the right color.

Third Lady: Catherine, your ball of silk is the color the tailors are looking for! Bring it to the king, and you can ask what you like for it.

Narrator: Catherine, looking quite beautiful in her best clothes, went to the court.

Catherine: Your Majesty, I have brought you a ball of silk of the color you need. I think you'll find that it is perfect for your wedding clothes.

King: Thank you! You shall have its weight in gold in return for bringing it to me.

From *Multicultural Folktales: Readers Theatre for Elementary Students.* © 2000 Suzanne I. Barchers. Teacher Ideas Press. 1-800-237-6124.

Narrator: The king's servant brought a pair of scales. A handful of gold was placed in one scale and the ball of silk in the other. But the silk was heavier. The king added more gold, but the silk still outweighed the gold. Finally, he put his golden crown on the scale and the scales finally balanced.

King: Where did you get this silk?

Catherine: It was given to me by my mistress.

King: I don't believe you. You need to tell me the truth or face the consequences.

Narrator: So Catherine told him the whole story of how she lost her father and her way of life.

King: You have suffered much, my girl, but your luck has turned. You are more beautiful than all the ladies of the court, and I will marry no one else.

Narrator: And so it was that the king sent away his bride-to-be. He and Catherine came to be great friends. Soon she loved the king deeply and they were married, with the king wearing the silken clothes. As promised, Catherine lived a happy life until she died.

How Fisher Went to the Skyland

Great Lakes Region/Anishinabe

Summary

When Young Fisher goes out to hunt, Grandfather Squirrel tells him how to get his father to bring warm weather to Earth. Fisher, the father, goes to Skyland with Otter and Wolverine. He succeeds in part, and Earth remains cold half the year, warming during the other half. However, he doesn't escape the sky people, who turn Fisher into the Big Dipper. (Fisher is actually a foxlike animal that is closely related to weasels. Although named Fisher, the animal dislikes water and hunts squirrels and other small animals.)

Presentation Suggestions

The narrator has long passages. If preferred, designate a second narrator to share the parts. The narrator and Fisher should stand to the front of the stage. The other characters could stand for their parts, sitting when finished.

Props

The characters could wear signs indicating their names. A mural depicting the sky could provide a backdrop for the script.

Delivery Suggestions

The narrator should carefully rehearse the readings. The pace should be even and smooth, in the nature of Native American storytelling. The characters should deliver their lines in keeping with their roles.

Characters

Narrator	Otter
Squirrel	Lynx
Young Fisher	Wolverine
Mother	Sky People (two or more)
Fisher	

"How Fisher Went to the Skyland" was adapted from "How Fisher Went to the Skyland: The Origin of the Big Dipper" in *Keepers of the Earth: Native American Stories and Environmental Activities for Children* by Michael J. Caduto and Joseph Bruchac (Golden, CO: Fulcrum, 1988, 1989, 1997), 117–20. Used with permission.

How Fisher Went to the Skyland

Narrator: Fisher was a great hunter. He wasn't big, but he was known for his determination. His son wanted to be a great hunter also. One day, the son went out to try to catch something. It wasn't easy, for the snow was very deep and it was cold everywhere. In those days, it was always winter on Earth and there was no such thing as warm weather. The son hunted a long time with no luck. Finally, though, he saw a grandfather Squirrel. Young Fisher sneaked up quietly and then pounced, catching Grandfather Squirrel between his paws. Just as Young Fisher was about to kill Squirrel, he spoke to Young Fisher.

Squirrel: Grandson, don't kill me. I can give you some good advice.

Young Fisher: Speak then.

Squirrel: I see that you are shivering from the cold. If you do as I tell you, we may all enjoy warm weather. Then it will be easy for all of us to find food and not starve as we are doing now.

Young Fisher: Tell me what to do, Grandfather.

Narrator: Grandfather Squirrel climbed quickly up onto a high branch before speaking.

Squirrel: Go home and say nothing. Just sit down in your lodge and begin to weep. Your mother will ask you what is wrong, but you must not answer her. If she tries to comfort you or give you food, you must refuse it. When your father comes home, he will ask you why you are weeping. Then you can speak. Tell him the winds are too cold and the snow is too deep. Tell him that he must bring warm weather to Earth.

Narrator: So Young Fisher went home. He sat in the corner of the lodge and cried.

Mother: Son, why are you crying?

Narrator: But Young Fisher just kept crying.

Mother: Son, let me fix you something to eat.

Narrator: But Young Fisher refused to eat. Finally, his father came home.

Fisher: What is wrong, son?

Young Fisher: I am weeping because the wind is too cold and the snow is too deep. We are all starving because of the winter. I want you to use your powers to bring the warm weather.

Fisher: What you are asking for is hard for me to do. But you are right. I will do all I can to grant your wish.

Narrator: Then Fisher had a great feast. He invited all his friends and told them what he planned to do.

Fisher: I am going to go to the place where the Skyland is closest to Earth. The people there have all the warm weather. I intend to bring some of that warm weather back. Then the snow will go away and we will have plenty to eat.

Narrator: All of Fisher's friends were pleased and offered to go with him. So when Fisher set out, he took the strongest of his friends along. They were Otter, Lynx, and Wolverine. The four of them traveled for a long time through the snow. They went toward the mountains, climbing higher and higher each day. Fisher brought along a pack filled with dried venison, and they slept at night buried under the snow. At last, after many, many days, they came to the highest mountain and climbed to its top. Then Fisher took a pipe and tobacco out of his pouch.

Fisher: We must offer our smoke to the Four Directions.

Narrator: The four of them smoked and sent their prayers to Gitchee Manitou, asking for success. The sky was very close above them, but they had to find some way to break through into the land above.

Fisher: We must jump up. Who will go first?

Otter: I will try.

Narrator: Otter leaped up and struck the sky, but did not break through. Instead, he fell back and slid on his belly all the way to the bottom of the mountain. To this day, all otters slide like that in the snow.

Lynx: Now it is my turn.

Narrator: Lynx jumped too, striking hard against the sky and falling back unconscious. Fisher tried then, but even he did not have enough power.

Wolverine: I will try now, for I am the strongest.

Narrator: Wolverine leaped and struck hard against the sky. He fell back, but he did not give up. He leaped again and again until he had made a crack in the sky. Once more he leaped and finally broke through. Fisher jumped through the hole in the sky after him.

Beautiful Skyland was warm and sunny, and there were trees and flowers of all kinds growing. They could hear the singing of birds all around them, but they could see no people. They went farther and found many long lodges. When they looked inside, they found cages in the lodges. Each cage held a different bird.

Fisher: These will make for fine hunting. Let us set them free.

Narrator: Quickly, Wolverine and Fisher chewed through the rawhide that bound the cages together and freed the birds. They all flew down through the hole in the sky, giving the world many birds. Wolverine and Fisher began to make the hole in Skyland bigger. The warmth of the Skyland began to fall through the hole, and the land below grew warmer. The snow began to melt and the grass and plants beneath the snow turned green. But the sky people came out when they saw what was happening. They ran toward Wolverine and Fisher.

Sky People: Thieves! Stop taking our warm weather!

Narrator: Wolverine jumped back through the hole to escape, but Fisher kept making the hole bigger. He knew that if he didn't make it big enough, the sky people would quickly close the hole again and it would be winter again in the land below. He chewed the hole larger and larger. Finally, just when the sky people were very close, he stopped.

The hole was big enough for enough warm weather for half the year to escape through, but it was not big enough for warm weather to last all the time. That is why the winter comes back every year. Fisher knew that the sky people might try to close the hole in the sky. He had to take their attention away from it, and so he taunted them.

Fisher: I am Fisher, the great hunter. You can't catch me!

Narrator: Fisher ran to the tallest tree in Skyland. All the sky people ran after him. Just as they were about to grab him, he leaped up into the tree and climbed to the highest branches, where no one could follow.

Sky People: Let's get our arrows. We'll shoot him down!

Narrator: They shot their arrows at Fisher, but he wasn't hurt, for he had a special power. There was only one place on his tail where an arrow could kill him. Finally, though, they guessed where his magic didn't work and shot at that place. An arrow struck the fatal spot. Fisher turned over on his back and began to fall.

But Fisher never struck Earth. Gitchee Manitou took pity on him because he had kept his promise and done something to help all the people. Gitchee Manitou placed Fisher high up in the sky among the stars.

If you look up into the sky, you can still see him, even though some people call that pattern of stars the Big Dipper. Every year he crosses the sky. When the arrow strikes him, he rolls over onto his back in the winter sky. But when the winter is almost ended, he faithfully turns to his feet and starts out once more on his long journey to bring the warm weather back to Earth.

Polly Ann and John Henry

United States

Summary

Polly Ann is setting fence posts when John Henry sweeps her off her feet. They marry and John Henry joins a steel-driving crew for the Chesapeake and Ohio Railroad. When the arrival of a steam drill machine threatens his livelihood, John Henry enters into a contest to prove that a man is more powerful than a machine.

Presentation Suggestions

The narrator plays an important role and should rehearse the script carefully. Because the parents speak only one line each, they could leave the stage after their parts. The machine salesman could enter the stage late in the story.

Props

John Henry could wear a railroad or workman's cap. A sledgehammer, fencing materials, and other tools could be propped onstage.

Delivery Suggestions

The spoken parts are written in a casual style. The characters should sound folksy without sounding ignorant.

Characters

Narrator
Mama
Papa
Polly Ann
John Henry
Captain Tommy
Men
Machine Salesman

Polly Ann and John Henry

Narrator: When Polly Ann arrived in this world, the Moon moved in front of the Sun for five full minutes. Her parents took this to mean that Polly Ann would be truly special.

Mama: You were so fine the Sun winked at the world. Child, there's nothing you can't do!

Narrator: Polly Ann believed her mama. When other little girls played with their dollies, Polly Ann practiced pounding nails into wood scraps from her papa's shop. While her cousins had tea parties, Polly Ann pitched horseshoes with her papa.

Papa: My pretty Polly! How you can pound a nail and pitch a horseshoe! You make me proud!

Narrator: With all that pounding and pitching, Polly Ann grew to be one strong young lady. Pretty, too. Fellas would come calling. But it wouldn't take long for those unsuspecting young men to decide that anyone who could pitch a game like Polly Ann would not make a good housewife. One hot day, Polly Ann was about to start a new fence down by the road. Just as she was fixing to set the gate post, up sauntered a young man as handsome as the night and looking twice as strong.

John Henry: Looks like you could use some help, miss.

Narrator: Polly Ann looked the young man square in the eyes, hoisted her hammer, and set that post with one blow.

Polly Ann: Thanks anyway, but I rather enjoy setting posts.

John Henry: Then maybe you'd be so kind as to fetch me a dipper of water. It is mighty hot today.

Polly Ann: Help yourself. What's your name?

John Henry: My name's John Henry. And yours?

Polly Ann: Polly Ann. Where you from and where you headed?

John Henry: Yonder the next county, but now I'm off to find the new railroad. I've a hankering to pound some steel.

Polly Ann: But you've got no hammer.

John Henry: I reckon I'll just have to use yours, Miss Polly Ann.

From *Multicultural Folktales: Readers Theatre for Elementary Students.* © 2000 Suzanne I. Barchers. Teacher Ideas Press. 1-800-237-6124.

Narrator: And that's how Polly Ann and John Henry commenced to courting. It took only two games of horseshoes to see that they were fairly matched. John Henry suggested they finish that new fence together. By the time they set the third post, they were in love. By the seventh post they were engaged. By the time the last post was pounded into place, the wedding date was set. After the wedding, John Henry was ready to move on.

John Henry: It's time to find that railroad, Polly Ann. We'll have a fine honeymoon on our way.

Narrator: John Henry and Polly Ann headed west until they came to the Big Bend Tunnel of the Chesapeake and Ohio Railroad. Hearing the men hammering and singing as they worked made John Henry eager to join them. It didn't take long for him to find the boss.

John Henry: Captain Tommy! I would surely like to sign on as a steel-driving man!

Captain Tommy: I don't know about that. That's a mighty big job. You don't even have a hammer.

John Henry: I've got hers.

Men: A girl's hammer? What kind of man is he?

Narrator: Just to prove that he could do the job, Polly Ann gave over her hammer and stood in as John Henry's shaker, setting each spike in place for John Henry to hit. In no time, she was calling for a bucket of water to cool down that fast-moving hammer.

Captain Tommy: You're hired! You'll get a dollar a day, a house to borrow, and your vittles. You can start right now!

Narrator: John Henry and Polly Ann settled down, happy as fleas on a dog. Before long, Polly Ann and John Henry had a little one, John Henry Junior. They put every spare penny into the cookie jar for the day when they could have their own place. Then one day, a man came along bragging about a new-fangled machine called a steam drill.

Machine Salesman: This machine never stops! It can do the work of twenty men! Just try it out, Captain Tommy. You won't regret buying it.

Captain Tommy: I have a hard time believing your claims. But, I tell you what, how about a race between that machine and my best natural-born machine, John Henry? If John Henry wins, you give me that machine and two hundred dollars. If the machine wins, I'll buy it from you.

Machine Salesman: Sounds fair enough, if your natural-born steel driver is willing!

From *Multicultural Folktales: Readers Theatre for Elementary Students.* © 2000 Suzanne I. Barchers. Teacher Ideas Press. 1-800-237-6124.

Captain Tommy: John Henry, I'll give you one hundred dollars if you can beat that machine.

John Henry: You don't have to talk me into it. If that machine takes over, where are hard-working, natural-born folks like me going to find jobs?

Narrator: They set the day for the contest, and people from a hundred miles away came to watch.

Polly Ann: John Henry, I know you feel you got to do this, but I won't be the same if anything happens to you.

John Henry: Polly Ann, a man ain't nothing but a man. And a man's always got to do his best. I'll beat that machine, just you wait and see. That hundred dollars can buy us our own place.

Narrator: The contest began. At first the steam-powered machine pulled ahead. But John Henry just grabbed a hammer in his other hand and worked harder and faster. He sang as he worked, knowing he could beat that machine. Every hour they had to call in a new shaker to keep up with all the spikes John Henry drove. The machine worked hard, too. But after eight hours, it began to shake just a little. John Henry just kept driving with both hammers, but he was getting weary, and there were no shakers left. Polly Ann pushed past the men in the tunnel and took over as the shaker.

Polly Ann: John Henry, you're going to win. You're a natural-born, steel-driving man.

Narrator: Polly Ann kept setting those spikes as her eyes burned from the dust and smarted from the tears at watching the man she loved drive those spikes. Finally, during the ninth and last hour, the machine began to overheat. Polly Ann and John Henry just kept setting and driving.

Men: Come on, John Henry! Don't give up! You can do it!

Captain Tommy: Time's up!

Narrator: The machine wheezed and died. John Henry began to drop the hammers, but Polly Ann took both his arms with hers and brought them down together on the last two spikes. The crowd listened as that one last furious ring of the hammers echoed throughout the tunnel, and then quiet settled in the tunnel. The dust cleared and the men saw that John Henry had indeed won—by three spikes! They also saw that he lay on the ground. Polly Ann was holding him in her arms, with her tears washing the dust from his face.

John Henry: Did we win, Polly Ann?

Polly Ann: You won, John Henry. We're gonna' go buy that place with our hundred dollars.

John Henry: Just give me a cool drink of water, and I'll be ready to move on. I'm fine Polly Ann.

Narrator: But before anyone could fetch him a drink, he had moved on forever. Polly Ann picked him up and carried him outside the tunnel and right up to their little home. A few days later, she and Junior buried John Henry on the hillside with her hammer in his hand and a steel rod across his breast. The clouds moved across the sun for five whole minutes, and the earth trembled as if a train were roaring down the tracks.

Polly Ann stayed on for a while, working to complete that tunnel. Some days she'd drive steel. Other days she'd be a shaker. But memories of John Henry became too much for her. She took that hundred dollars, plus all her cookie jar savings, and headed west with Junior. They got that place, and every time she set a fence post with her new hammer she'd think about her natural-born, steel-driving man and tell their son how his daddy beat a new-fangled machine.

Princess Sivatra

India

Summary

When Princess Sivatra falls in love with young Sayavan, she is dismayed to learn that he will die within a year. She marries him anyway, but when the year draws to a close she pleads with the gods for his life. When death comes, her persistence saves Sayavan and restores his father to his throne and former good health.

Presentation Suggestions

Sivatra should have a central role, with her father on one side of her and Sayavan on the other. To add dramatic effect, Yama can enter the stage when his lines begin.

Props

A mural could suggest a quiet forest scene. Sivatra could be dressed in regal but simple clothing. Sayavan should be dressed in work clothes. Yama could be dressed in long, dark robes, symbolizing death.

Delivery Suggestions

Sivatra should sound determined and wise. The king should sound devoted and understanding. Yama should be threatening at first and then exasperated as Sivatra continues to press him for additional wishes.

Characters

Narrator
Sivatra
King
Counselor
Sayavan
Yama

Princess Sivatra

Narrator: Once there was an honorable king of a region of India who was loved by his people. He would have been completely happy, except that he had no children. The goddess Siva took pity on him. She told him that he would have a daughter by the end of the year. When the baby arrived, the king named her Sivatra in honor of the goddess Siva. Soon Sivatra turned eighteen. It was time for her to journey into the forest to learn from those who lived there in peace and harmony. When she returned, she went to her father.

Sivatra: Father, while I was in the forest, I met the exiled king Yumatsena. His enemies left him poor and blind. He lives with his son Sayavan.

King: I know them both, dear. They are fine people who have seen hard times.

Sivatra: Father, there is more. I have fallen in love with Sayavan and request permission to marry him.

King: This is an unfortunate, though noble, family, daughter. Let me consult my counselor to see if this match is wise.

Narrator: The king called his counselor and told him about Sivatra's request.

Counselor: My noble king, I regret what I must tell you. Last night, the goddess Siva came to me in a dream. Sayavan has only one year to live.

King: Are you sure?

Counselor: Sivatra faces terrible grief if she marries Sayavan.

Narrator: The king sadly called his daughter to him.

King: Sivatra, I am afraid this match is not wise. Sayavan will die soon. You would be left a young widow. Find yourself a healthy man.

Sivatra: Father, it doesn't matter to me how much time we have together. An hour of happiness with Sayavan is worth more to me than a lifetime with another.

King: How can I deny you anything, my daughter? You have my permission to marry.

Narrator: Sivatra and Sayavan married in the forest where they had met. A year seemed a long time to them. But they were so happy the days raced by. Soon only four days were left of the year. Sivatra decided to appeal to the gods. She went to the forest and stood in the place where they had met. Sayavan, unaware of his fate, came in search of her.

Sayavan: Sivatra, why are you standing in the forest?

Sivatra: My love, I cannot tell you more than this. I will be standing here for four days and nights. I must do this as an offering to the gods. That is all I can say.

Sayavan: Please tell me why you are doing this. I don't understand this at all.

Narrator: But Sivatra would not explain. She whispered to the gods that she would pray until Sayavan was saved. Soon the last sun peeked over the horizon. Sayavan, not realizing that this was his last day, came to plead with his wife.

Sayavan: Sivatra, you have not eaten or slept for four days and nights. Let me take you home to rest. Then I will gather some sweet fruit for you to eat.

Sivatra: Dear Sayavan, my greatest wish is to have this day with you. Let us go gather the fruit together.

Narrator: Sayavan and Sivatra walked quietly through the forest. After they had gathered some fruit, Sivatra rested while Sayavan collected some firewood. She continued to pray to the gods that Sayavan would be spared. Suddenly, Sayavan returned.

Sayavan: Sivatra, my head hurts terribly. I must rest.

Narrator: Sayavan fell into a deep sleep. Sivatra drew his head onto her lap and watched him sleep. Suddenly, a huge figure appeared before her. She stood to face it.

Sivatra: Who are you? You are not of this world, are you?

Yama: I am Yama, god of the dead. I am here for your husband.

Narrator: Sayavan took his last breath. Yama turned to leave with Sayavan's soul. Sivatra ran past Yama and stood in his path.

Yama: Be gone with you! His life is done.

Sivatra: My life is with Sayavan. I will follow him—and you—wherever you go.

Yama: I can't give you back his life. But I can give you a wish. What would it be?

Sivatra: Sayavan's father is blind. Can you give him back his sight?

Yama: Consider it done. Now go.

Narrator: But Sivatra would not move.

Yama: I will grant you another wish. What is it?

Sivatra: Sayavan's father has been exiled for many years. Give him back his empire.

Yama: It is done. Now move away.

From *Multicultural Folktales: Readers Theatre for Elementary Students*. © 2000 Suzanne I. Barchers. Teacher Ideas Press. 1-800-237-6124.

Narrator: Though Sivatra was weak with fatigue, she held her ground.

Yama: You are so determined. I'll grant you a third wish. What would it be?

Sivatra: My father has no son. Give him a son.

Yama: As you wish. Now leave me to my task.

Narrator: But Sivatra continued to stand in Yama's path.

Yama: All right, you may have a fourth wish.

Sivatra: I want a son.

Yama: You shall have a son, but now you must let me by. Return to your home.

Narrator: Yama pushed her aside and headed down the path. But in spite of her weariness, Sivatra followed behind.

Sivatra: Please grant me one last wish.

Yama: You are most annoying, but I admire your devotion. I'll grant you one last wish.

Narrator: Yama was so tired of facing her that he granted her wish without thinking what it meant. Then he disappeared. Sivatra ran back to her husband and cradled his head in her arms. His color began to return, and his eyes fluttered open.

Sayavan: What happened? Have I been asleep?

Sivatra: You were only resting a bit, my dear. Let's go home.

Narrator: The tired young couple walked slowly through the forest. As they returned to their home they learned that Sayavan's father could see once again. Next, they learned that the enemy king had been overthrown.

King: This is a night of miracles!

Narrator: Sivatra thought of all that had happened. She had not lost Sayavan. But she knew she would treasure every moment she had with him for the rest of their lives.

The Three Wishes

Hungary

Summary

When a poor man helps a fairy get her carriage out of the mud, she tells the poor man that his wife can have three wishes. The poor man tells his wife of their good fortune, and she immediately wishes for a sausage for their dinner. They realize that they had better be careful with the other wishes, anticipating becoming rich. But when the man upsets the pan and sausage, the wife becomes annoyed and wishes the sausage were on his nose. After some argument, they use their last wish to remove the sausage.

Presentation Suggestions

The characters have equally important roles and can be spaced across the stage in a line.

Props

The little woman could be wearing a fancy dress. The man and his wife should be dressed poorly. The setting could be a simple kitchen.

Delivery Suggestions

The husband should sound deferential when talking with the little woman. Then he should be excited and finally exasperated at his wife. The wife should vary her delivery, sounding alternately excited and vexed.

Characters

Narrator
Man
Little Woman
Wife

The Three Wishes

Narrator: One day, a poor man was walking home along a muddy road. He saw a little woman sitting in a carriage pulled by four little dogs. It was stuck in the mud, and the woman was afraid to get out.

Man: Your carriage seems to be quite stuck. Can I help you?

Little Woman: I would be so very grateful for your help.

Man: I'll be glad to give you a push.

Narrator: The man helped the dogs and soon they had the carriage free.

Little Woman: Thank you for your help. Are you married, young man?

Man: Yes, I have a fine wife at home.

Little Woman: Are you rich then?

Man: Oh, no, I am almost the poorest in the village.

Little Woman: Well, I can help you improve your lot! I will grant your fine wife three wishes.

Narrator: Before the man could thank her, she was gone. He realized that she must have been a fairy. He hurried home to his wife.

Man: Wife, the most amazing thing has happened! As I was coming from the field, I saw a carriage with a little woman inside. Four dogs were pulling it, but it was stuck fast in the mud. The woman didn't want to get out and soil her dress, so I offered to help. After the dogs and I got the carriage out, she said that you could have three wishes!

Wife: What good luck for us! You know I wish we had some sausage to cook on our fire.

Narrator: Before they could blink, a huge sausage appeared in a frying pan on the fire.

Wife: What a wonderful sausage! But we should be careful with the other two wishes. If we are clever, we can be rich and could even buy a cow, a horse, and a pig!

Narrator: The man sat back happily and began to fill his pipe as he warmed himself by the fire. Then he reached to the fire to light his pipe, upsetting the frying pan and the sausage.

Wife: Good heavens, look at what you are doing! I wish that sausage were on your nose!

Narrator: In a twinkling, that sausage was indeed hanging from the man's nose!

Man: Look what you have done! Now the second wish is gone! Such foolishness!

Wife: Can't we get it off?

Man: Don't you see? It's quite stuck!

Wife: Let's cut it off then.

Man: I'm afraid it is growing from my nose! There is only one thing left to do with that remaining wish. You had better wish that the sausage would go back in the pan.

Wife: But what about the cow, horse, and pig?

Man: Well, I can't go about with this sausage hanging from my nose, can I?

Narrator: They argued for a long time, but she finally wished that the sausage would go back to the pan. They were as poor as ever, but they made a good meal of the sausage. They did learn an important lesson, however. They agreed never to fight again. They kept their bargain and one day had their cow, horse, and pig, just as they had hoped.

To the Sun, Moon, and Wind

Spain

Summary

A young woman disobeys her new husband and peeks into a chest. When her husband and home disappear, she must journey to the Sun, Moon, and Wind to find her way to him. With the help of some magic, she uses her wit and perseverance to rescue her husband.

Presentation Suggestions

The narrator provides background and direction to the story and should rehearse carefully. The young woman's role is also pivotal. Other characters have relatively small roles and could exit or sit down after reading their parts.

Props

The stage could be enhanced with a plant, farming implements, or chest. Symbols of the Sun, Moon, and Wind could be hung as a backdrop.

Delivery Suggestions

The delivery should be in normal voices, giving expression to the parts as appropriate to the roles. The Sun, Moon, and Wind could be read by boys or girls.

Characters

Narrator
Young Man
Young Woman
Old Woman
Sun
Moon
Wind
Princess

From Multicultural Folktales: Readers Theatre for Elementary Students. © 2000 Suzanne I. Barchers. Teacher Ideas Press. 1-800-237-6124.

To the Sun, Moon, and Wind

Narrator: Once there was a man who made his daughter work very hard all day long. One day, the daughter was gathering leaves and twigs for kindling when she happened upon a rosemary plant. She decided to take a sprig of it home, but when she pulled at it, she pulled up the entire plant. A young man suddenly appeared.

Young Man: Why are you stealing my firewood?

Young Woman: I'm sorry, sir. My father sent me to gather wood, and I wanted a sprig of this rosemary plant to brighten our home.

Young Man: Come with me. I want to show you what you have uncovered.

Narrator: The young woman, being rather curious, followed him through the opening made by the uprooted rosemary plant. They traveled underground, visiting and getting acquainted, until they came to a splendid palace.

Young Man: I need to tell you the truth now. I am actually a lord and I have taken a fancy to you. Would you consider becoming my wife?

Narrator: The young woman had had such a difficult life that she decided living in such luxury would be a welcome change. She agreed to his offer, and soon the young couple was married.

Young Man: Now that you are my wife, it is time for you to have the keys to the castle. However, you are never to open the large oak chest in the last room. If you do, everything will be ruined for us.

Narrator: The young woman promised, but her curiosity got the better of her once again and she peeked into the chest. When she opened the chest she found a serpent's skin. She didn't know that her husband was a magician who used the skin for his sorcery. Before she could close the chest, the earth trembled, the palace vanished, and she found herself in the middle of a field.

Young Woman: Why have I been so foolish! Everything is gone but the rosemary plant.

Narrator: She decided to take a sprig of rosemary and search the world until she found her husband and begged his forgiveness. Soon she came to a small house in the nearby village.

Young Woman: Excuse me, ma'am. I am in need of work and would beg that you give me some chores so that I can earn some food.

Old Woman: I can see that you need help, but what is troubling you so?

From *Multicultural Folktales: Readers Theatre for Elementary Students.* © 2000 Suzanne I. Barchers. Teacher Ideas Press. 1-800-237-6124.

Young Woman: I was very foolish, ma'am. I was married to a wonderful man, but I disobeyed him. I am determined to search the world until I find him.

Old Woman: I can't help you find him, but I can give you some advice. You need to go to the Sun, the Moon, and the Wind and ask where he is. They go everywhere and know what is happening in the world. Take this food and continue your search.

Young Woman: You are most kind, and I will accept your advice gladly.

Narrator: The young woman set out and soon knocked on the door of the golden castle of the Sun.

Young Woman: Oh, Sun, I have come to ask for your help. Through my own foolishness I have lost my husband. I know you see almost everything. Can you tell me where he is?

Sun: I can't tell you where he is, but here is a nut. It is magical, but you must open it only when you are in great need.

Young Woman: Thank you, Sun, but what should I do now?

Sun: Go to Moon and see if Moon can tell you where he is.

Narrator: The girl searched and searched, and finally she came to the silver castle of the Moon.

Young Woman: Dear Moon, I disobeyed my husband and gave in to my curiosity. Now I have lost him. Can you help me find him?

Moon: I haven't seen your husband, but I can give you this walnut. Its magic will help you, but only if you use it when you are in great need.

Young Woman: Thank you, Moon. Can you be so kind as to direct me to Wind?

Moon: Just follow your heart, my dear. Many times Wind comes to you.

Narrator: The young woman did exactly as Moon directed her and soon came to Wind's castle, high on a hill. She was so distressed that she wept as she talked to Wind.

Young Woman: At last I have found you, Wind. Can you help me find my husband? I was foolish and lost him forever.

Wind: I have not seen your husband, but I will take a quick look around. Wait right here.

Narrator: Wind blustered through the world and soon returned to the young woman.

Wind: I have learned something of great importance. Your husband is under a spell that has made him forget you. He is in the palace of a king who intends to marry him to his ill-tempered daughter.

Young Woman: Can you help me, dear Wind? Can you delay the wedding until I can get there?

Wind: I'll see what I can do, but don't delay! Here is an almond that will help you when you need it most.

Narrator: While the young woman made her way to the palace, Wind whisked off and made mischief with the tailors who were trying to complete the bridal costume. Wind scattered all the ribbons and laces, blowing them out the windows. The king agreed to delay the ceremony until the tailors could complete new costumes. Finally, the young woman arrived at the castle. Before she knocked on the door, she cracked the first nut, and a beautiful veil appeared. She asked to see the princess.

Young Woman: Princess, would you like this veil for the wedding?

Princess: That is a wonderful veil. How much do you want for it?

Narrator: The princess gladly paid the price and went in the castle. The young woman cracked open the walnut, and some exquisite petticoats appeared. She asked for the princess again.

Young Woman: Princess, would you also like to have these petticoats for your wedding?

Princess: They are truly the most beautiful I have seen. I'll gladly pay you for them.

Narrator: They settled on a price, and the princess left. Then the young woman opened up the almond, and a dress of great brilliance appeared. She asked to see the princess again.

Young Woman: Princess, would you like to have this dress for your wedding?

Princess: This is amazing! I can't live without this dress! How much do you want?

Young Woman: I have just one request. I would like to see your groom.

Narrator: This didn't please the princess, but she dearly wanted the dress and felt she had no choice but to agree. The young woman, still carrying her sprig of rosemary, was led to where her husband was sleeping. She touched him with the sprig of rosemary, and the spell was broken. He woke up, rejoicing in seeing her again. They called for the king and told him that they were truly husband and wife. After their journey home, they lived happily together for the rest of their lives.

The Young Chief Who Played the Flute

New Zealand

Summary

A young Maori chief, Tutanekai, falls in love with Hinemoa, who lives on another island. Forbidden to marry, Hinemoa listens to Tutanekai's flute music every night. Finally, she decides to risk her life by swimming across to Tutanekai's island. She tricks a servant by breaking Tutanekai's calabashes and he finally comes to find out who the troublemaker is. They marry and play wonderful music together.

Presentation Suggestions

The narrator, Tutanekai, and Hinemoa have the central roles. They should stand in the center of the stage. The brothers can leave or sit down after their lines.

Props

If possible, obtain a recorder or simple reed flute to place onstage. A mural showing the ocean and two islands could serve as a backdrop. The islanders could be dressed in simple clothing with bright colors.

Delivery Suggestions

The participants should practice their parts carefully so that they can pronounce the names and unfamiliar words smoothly. When Hinemoa is at the hot pool pretending to be a man, she should use a deep voice. Other characters should use normal voices.

Characters

Narrator

First Brother

Second Brother

Hinemoa

Tutanekai

Servant

"The Young Chief Who Played the Flute" was adapted from "The Young Chief Who Played the Flute" in *Troubadour's Storybag: Musical Folktales of the World*, retold and edited by Norma J. Livo (Golden, CO: Fulcrum, 1996), 51–55. Used with permission.

The Young Chief Who Played the Flute

Narrator: A young chief named Tutanekai lived on a New Zealand island, Mokoia. He lived there with the Maoris. He and his brothers enjoyed hearing many stories about Hinemoa, the beautiful young woman who lived in the village of Owhata. They decided they were in love with her, even though they had never seen her.

First Brother: I'm going to marry her one day!

Second Brother: Not you, brother! She is so gentle and beautiful. I will have her for my own.

Narrator: Only Tutanekai said nothing. But in the evenings he would go to the top of the hillside and look across the water toward Owhata. He would take out his flute and play songs of love. Sometimes Hinemoa heard these songs as she sat in the moonlight. She had heard stories about the brothers of Mokoia.

Hinemoa: That must be Tutanekai playing the flute. He plays beautifully.

Narrator: Soon it was festival time. The people of Mokoia visited Owhata. Tutanekai was among them and he soon saw the beautiful Hinemoa. She recognized him as the handsome flute player. She nodded at him, motioning toward the side of the meeting house. Later, they met and talked.

Tutanekai: I have waited so long to meet you. When can we meet again?

Hinemoa: I will come to you. My people won't let me marry you, but I will try to come when I can. How will I know you are waiting for me?

Tutanekai: You have heard my music of love. Now when you hear it, you will know I am still waiting for you.

Narrator: The people left the next morning. That night, Hinemoa slipped down to the beach and looked for a small canoe. She knew she could paddle to the island. But all the canoes were dragged high up on the beach. They were too heavy for her to move. She spoke to herself.

Hinemoa: The old people must have seen how Tutanekai and I looked at each other. They are trying to make sure I don't go to him.

Narrator: Hinemoa heard the sound of the flute and knew that Tutanekai was waiting for her. She sadly returned to her house. The next night, she returned to the beach, only to find the canoes dragged high on the beach. Night after night she returned to the beach, only to listen to Tutanekai's flute playing.

Hinemoa: How long will Tutanekai wait for me? If only there were a way to get across the water.

Narrator: Finally, Hinemoa decided that she would try to swim across. She tied some empty gourds under her arms and waded out into the water. The music came across the water to guide her, but the waves made it hard to hear. The water was cold. She became frightened and lost. But she kept swimming. The music stopped, but she could hear waves on a rocky shore. She swam to the beach and found herself at a hot pool near Tutanekai's home. She spread her clothes out to dry and then stepped into the hot pool to warm herself. Suddenly, she heard footsteps. She disguised her voice to sound like a man.

Hinemoa: Who are you? What are you doing here?

Servant: I am taking water to Tutanekai.

Hinemoa: Give me the calabash!

Narrator: Hinemoa took the calabash and threw it on the rocks. It broke into a hundred pieces.

Servant: Why did you do that?

Narrator: But Hinemoa had stayed well hidden and the servant couldn't find her. He went back to tell Tutanekai what had happened.

Servant: Master, there was someone at the pool. He took the calabash and broke it.

Tutanekai: Who was this?

Servant: I couldn't see, but he sounded like a man.

Narrator: Tutanekai thought of going down to the pool himself. But all he could think about was Hinemoa. Had she forgotten him?

Tutanekai: It doesn't matter about the calabash. Take another one to the hot pool. Bring it back full this time.

Narrator: The servant returned to the hot pool. Once again, he heard the deep voice.

Hinemoa: If that is Tutanekai's calabash, give it to me!

Servant: No! I must take it back to Tutanekai.

Hinemoa: Give it to me!

Narrator: The servant was frightened and gave her the calabash. Once again, she broke it.

Servant: The second calabash is gone, too. It was the same man who took it and smashed it.

Tutanekai: Never mind. We have plenty of calabashes. Take another and try again.

Narrator: Once again, Hinemoa demanded and destroyed the calabash. This time, Tutanekai got angry and decided to go to the hot pool himself. Hinemoa heard him coming and knew who it was. She hid behind a rock.

Tutanekai: Where are you? Why do you break my calabashes? Come out so that I can see you!

Narrator: Tutanekai saw her hair and took hold of it, thinking he had caught the rascal. He pulled while she stood up slowly and shyly. Tutanekai looked at her in amazement. They went up the path to his home and were married soon after. From that day on, Hinemoa and Tutanekai enjoyed the music of the flute together.

Chapter 5

Fifth-Grade Reading Level

139

The Doomed Prince

Egypt

Summary

In this tale from Egypt, a young prince is doomed from birth to die from a crocodile, serpent, or dog. Despite the king's efforts to shield him, the prince sets out on his own. He meets and marries a chief's daughter, but returns to Egypt with his wife. En route, his life is threatened by a serpent, but his vigilant wife saves him. As he is being carried away by a crocodile, the story ends abruptly. Adapted from a story found on the Harris Papyrus in the British Museum, the story is left unfinished because the papyrus was torn and the ending was lost. The papyrus is said to date from the Eighteenth Dynasty, about 1700 B.C.

Presentation Suggestions

The narrator and prince have the primary roles and should stand in prominent positions on the stage. The Hathors and attendant have only one line each and could leave after reading their lines.

Props

An Egyptian motif would enhance the script. Consider decorating a mural with pyramids, having a scroll with hieroglyphics, or adding statuary or vases. Students could research Egyptian dress and create simple costumes.

Delivery Suggestions

The characters can deliver their lines in normal voices.

Characters

Narrator
Hathors (two or more students)
Prince
Attendant
King
Chief
Chief's Daughter

The Doomed Prince

Narrator: There was once a king who was sad because he had no son. Finally, his wife had a son. The Hathors came to decide his destiny. Their decree was not a happy one.

Hathors: Your son's death shall be by the crocodile, by the serpent, or by the dog.

Narrator: The king was upset upon hearing this and decided to build a house that housed everything a child might want. He thought he could ensure that his son would never want to go abroad. One day, the young prince saw something from the roof of the house.

Prince: What is that which follows the man coming along the road?

Attendant: Your Majesty, that is a dog.

Prince: Tell my father that I want to have a dog.

Narrator: When the king heard of his son's desire, he could not deny him. After many years, the prince grew restless. He went to speak with his father.

Prince: Father, why am I kept a prisoner?

King: Son, when you were born, the Hathors said that you would meet death by a crocodile, a serpent, or a dog. I have only tried to keep you safe from harm.

Prince: Father, though I am destined to one of three evil fates, let me follow my desires.

King: All right, son, but please take great care.

Narrator: The prince was given weapons and allowed to take his faithful dog as he headed north, following whatever path appealed to him. Finally, he came to the home of the chief of Nahairana. This chief had only one daughter, and he had built a house with seventy windows, seventy cubits from the ground. Before the prince arrived, the chief had commanded that all the sons of the chiefs of the country of Khalu be brought. He had then issued a decree.

Chief: He who climbs and reaches my daughter's windows shall win her for his wife.

Narrator: When the prince arrived, he was pleased to become acquainted with some people who befriended him. He didn't want them to know of his noble background, so he made up a fictitious life to tell them.

Prince: I come from Egypt, the son of an officer of that land. After my mother died, my father took another wife who, when she had other children, grew to hate me. Therefore, I fled from her presence and am a fugitive.

Narrator: His new friends accepted his story and welcomed him into their lives. One day, the prince noticed some youths climbing the chief's house. The prince asked them what they were doing and when the youths told him, he decided to accept the challenge. The prince quickly reached the daughter's window, where she welcomed him with an embrace. A messenger told the chief that a youth had climbed to his daughter's window. When the chief inquired as to who the young man was, the chief was told the young man was a fugitive from Egypt.

Chief: I'll not have my daughter marrying an Egyptian fugitive! He can return to his home!

Narrator: When the chief's daughter heard, she refused to let him go.

Chief's Daughter: If he is taken from me, I will neither eat nor drink and in that hour I will die!

Narrator: When the chief heard of her vow, he decided to send someone to slay the youth in his house. But his daughter had another threat.

Chief's Daughter: If he is slain, I will die before the sun sets. If we are parted, I will live no longer.

Narrator: When the chief heard her latest threat, he gave in and had his daughter and the youth brought before him.

Chief: Tell me who you are, for you are now like a son to me.

Prince: I come from Egypt, the son of an officer of that land. After my mother died, my father took another wife who, when she had other children, grew to hate me. Therefore, I fled from her presence and am a fugitive.

Narrator: The chief let them marry and gave them a house, lands, cattle, and all manner of good gifts. Years passed and finally the prince told his wife of his fate.

Prince: My dear, I fear that I am doomed. It was predicted that I would die by a crocodile, a serpent, or a dog.

Chief's Daughter: Then let someone kill your dog.

Prince: No, my dear, for I have brought that dog up since it was a puppy. But I yearn to return to Egypt.

Chief's Daughter: If you must go, then I will go with you.

Narrator: The young couple set out and one day came to a town where a great crocodile of the river lived. There was a mighty man there who would not let the crocodile escape. The prince became great friends with the crocodile's master. One night as the prince lay sleeping, his wife filled a bowl of milk and placed it by his side. A serpent came out from a hole and tried to bite the prince, but his wife was ready. She and the servants gave the serpent so much milk that it lay helpless on its back. Then she killed it with her dagger. The next morning, the prince saw what had happened.

Chief's Daughter: My dear, as you can see, you have escaped the serpent. Surely you shall escape the others as well.

Narrator: The prince rejoiced at having lived in spite of the threat of the serpent. One day thereafter, he was walking in the fields with his dog, who was chasing wild game. The dog plunged into the river, and the prince followed after him. Suddenly, the crocodile appeared, but he recognized the prince and began to take him back to the home of his master.

Now, dear listeners, the papyrus on which this tale was told was torn and the ending is unknown. What do you think happened? Did the crocodile devour him on the way? Did his dog lead him into even greater danger? The ending is for you to determine.

Fortunée

France

Summary

Orphaned and left to live with a mean brother, Fortunée's life improves when the Queen of the Woods befriends her. Fortunée tends her only belongings, a pot of pinks and a silver ring. Through the queen, she learns that she is truly a princess, the victim of unfortunate circumstances and an enchantment. The enchantment is broken and eventually she marries a prince.

Presentation Suggestions

Fortunée and the queen have the central roles and should be the central focus. The other characters can stand to one side or slightly to the back.

Props

Fortunée could be dressed simply, with the queen in elegant clothes. A plastic or stuffed hen and several cabbages could be on the stage. A table could hold a pot of pink flowers.

Delivery Suggestions

Fortunée should sound kind and sweet. The queen should sound regal. Bedou should sound mean. The hen could have a cackle, and the cabbage could sound like a gruff man.

Characters

Narrator
Bedou
Fortunée
Queen
Cabbage
Hen
Pinks

Fortunée

Narrator: Once upon a time there were two orphans whose father was very poor when he died. He had left his daughter Fortunée a silver ring and a pot of pinks that he had been given years before. The father had cared for them lovingly, and Fortunée tended them with great devotion. He left his son Bedou the remainder of his belongings. One day, Bedou came to see his sister.

Bedou: Fortunée, you have your ring and your flowers. Take care of them, but leave my house and belongings alone. They are mine and mine alone. You are lucky that I even let you live here.

Narrator: Fortunée was saddened by his cruelty. She went to her room where she kept her pot of pinks.

Fortunée: Dear flowers, I do enjoy your lovely color and smell. You are all I have, and I will always keep you safe.

Narrator: That evening, she took a jug to the stream to get the flowers some water. She saw a beautiful queen sitting at an ornate table covered with fine food.

Queen: Why are you out here all alone, my child? It's dangerous to be here by yourself.

Fortunée: You are kind to worry about me, Your Majesty, but I have nothing to steal. My father died and all I have is a silver ring and a pot of pinks.

Queen: But you do have a heart. Would you let your heart be stolen?

Fortunée: Your Majesty, without a heart I would die. Though I am poor, I do want to live.

Queen: You are indeed wise to defend your heart. Tell me, have you eaten tonight?

Fortunée: No, Your Majesty, my brother ate all our food.

Queen: Then you must eat with me.

Narrator: Fortunée sat with the queen, but she ate little. The queen was curious about her and continued to ask her questions.

Queen: Why did you come to the stream this evening?

Fortunée: I came to get water in my jug for my pinks.

Narrator: But when Fortunée reached for the jug, she discovered that it was now gold and encrusted with diamonds. Fragrant water filled the jug.

Queen: The jug is for you, Fortunée. Take care of your flowers and remember that the Queen of the Woods is now your friend.

Fortunée: You are so kind, Your Majesty. I thank you for this honor. If you will wait here, I would like to bring you half my flowers so that you could enjoy them as well.

Narrator: Fortunée ran home, carefully cradling the jug. At home, she found that Bedou had taken her flowers, leaving a cabbage in their place. She took her silver ring from its hiding place and returned to the queen.

Fortunée: Your Majesty, my brother took my flowers. All I have left is this ring. Please accept it instead of the flowers.

Queen: But it is all that you have.

Fortunée: No, Your Majesty, for I have your favor. That is all I need.

Narrator: The queen put on the ring and climbed into her jeweled carriage drawn by six magnificent horses. Fortunée watched as the queen rode away. When she returned home, she went to her room and threw the cabbage out the window.

Cabbage: You have killed me!

Narrator: Fortunée looked out her window, wondering who she had heard calling out. But she could see nothing. The next morning, she went into the garden and saw the cabbage again.

Fortunée: I wish I had my lovely flowers back. You are worth nothing to me.

Cabbage: I never wanted to be here! If you would kindly put me back in the vegetable garden where I belong, I can tell you where to find your pinks.

Fortunée: That is a fair enough trade. Here you are then, back home in your vegetable garden.

Cabbage: You'll find your pinks in Bedou's bed.

Narrator: Before Fortunée left the garden, she noticed Bedou's hen.

Fortunée: Hen, I should make you my dinner. That would serve Bedou right!

Hen: If you would spare me, I would tell you things you do not know.

Fortunée: And what would those be?

Hen: Just as I am not a hen, you are not the daughter of the man who raised you. Your mother was a queen who had six daughters. She was told she would be killed if her seventh child was also a girl. The queen's sister was a fairy who wanted to help. The queen had another daughter, but the fairy sister had a son. The fairy used her magic to send the babe on the wind to the queen, but the queen had become too frightened to wait. She ran away with the baby girl and came to this hut when I was still a poor woman. She gave you to me.

Fortunée: But then what happened?

Hen: She died, my dear, leaving me to raise you. But I couldn't resist talking about the queen who brought you to me. When I told this to a beautiful lady, she touched me with her wand and turned me into a hen. My husband thought I had been killed by one of the beasts in the forest. But one day, this lady returned and gave him the pot of pinks and the silver ring.

Fortunée: So that is why the pinks and ring were so precious to my father.

Hen: That's right, dear one. But the story is not done. While she was there, twenty-five of the king's soldiers came looking for you and your mother. The lady turned them all into cabbages, one of which you threw out the window last night. I had never heard one speak before. Indeed, this is the first time I have been able to speak.

Fortunée: I am sorry that you have suffered so much. Don't worry, though. I am going to look for my pinks. I believe that things will be better soon.

Narrator: Fortunée returned to the house and went directly to Bedou's room. She used the perfumed water on her pinks, enjoying the fragrance. Suddenly, she heard a voice coming from the flowers.

Pinks: Fortunée, you are so beautiful. I have to tell you of my love. Even these flowers bow to you.

Narrator: This was all becoming to much for Fortunée. First, a cabbage spoke to her and then a hen. Now a pot of pinks was declaring its love. Suddenly, Bedou appeared in his room.

Bedou: What are you doing in here? Get out! Get out of this house!

Narrator: Fortunée ran out of the house into the woods. The queen appeared before her.

Queen: Fortunée, your brother is a hateful person. Do you wish to have your revenge on him?

Fortunée: Your Majesty, I don't understand why he is so wicked, but I do not seek revenge. That would only make me like him.

Queen: But he is not your true brother. Haven't you been told you are a princess?

Fortunée: Yes, I have been told that. But until I have proof there is little I can do about it.

Queen: It is clear that your blood is noble. You are truly a princess, and I can now help you.

Narrator: Just then, a handsome prince appeared, dressed in rich clothing with a crown of pinks on his head. He knelt before the queen.

Queen: Dear one, your enchantment has come to an end, thanks to Fortunée. I know the hen has told you much, Fortunée, but what she did not know was that I was the fairy sister who sent her a son to be exchanged for you. When I sent him, the wind carried him to a flowerbed, and an evil fairy turned him into a pot of pinks. I arranged for you to care for the pot, knowing that my magic water would restore him. There is only one thing needed to break the enchantment forever. Could you find it in your heart to marry him?

Fortunée: Your Majesty, I could never agree to marry a man without knowing more of him and if he cared for me.

Pinks: Fortunée, I have loved you for years. You have shown your kindness in spite of the wickedness around you. If you will not have me for your husband, I will be content to be your pot of pinks once again. You can tend me as you have in the past.

Narrator: Fortunée was touched by his words and considered his request. The queen touched her with her wand, transforming her clothes into exquisite jeweled garments. Just then, Bedou came along, stopping in shock when he saw Fortunée looking like a princess. The queen was ready to punish Bedou for his evil treatment of Fortunée.

Fortunée: Your Majesty, please spare Bedou. I don't seek revenge.

Narrator: The queen was touched by her generous spirit. She turned Bedou's hut into a beautiful palace and changed his wickedness to kindness. Then she changed the cabbages back into men and the hen into a woman. Everyone was content for the moment except for the prince. He waited for many months while Fortunée considered whether she wanted him to court her. Finally, she agreed that he could call on her. At last they married and lived together for many happy years.

From *Multicultural Folktales: Readers Theatre for Elementary Students.* © 2000 Suzanne I. Barchers. Teacher Ideas Press. 1-800-237-6124.

The Forty Thieves

Arabia

Summary

While Ali Baba is chopping wood in the forest, he discovers a cave where great riches have been hidden by a band of thieves. He steals some gold, but his brother Cassim discovers the secret and tries to steal a fortune for himself. Cassim is killed by the robbers, who then try to kill Ali Baba. Thanks to the quick thinking of his servant, Morgiana, Ali Baba is saved. This version ends before the captain of the robbers seeks revenge. The students could research the story and create a sequel to this script.

Presentation Suggestions

The narrator has an important role and should stand toward the front and to one side. Ali Baba can stand next to the narrator. The other characters can range across the stage in order of their speaking roles, with the captain in a prominent position.

Props

Characters can dress in bright colors and sashes that represent Persia. If possible, decorate the stage with jars to suggest the jars of oil.

Delivery Suggestions

The narrator should practice the lines to provide a smooth delivery. Cassim should sound somewhat conniving. Captain should sound authoritative and sly.

Characters

Narrator
Captain
Ali Baba
Ali Baba's wife
Cassim's wife
Cassim
Morgiana
Apothecary
Thief
Cobbler

The Forty Thieves

Narrator: Two brothers lived in Persia. Cassim married a rich wife, enjoying a life of luxury. But Ali Baba, a poor man, cut wood in the nearby forest to support his wife and children. One day, Ali Baba was in the forest with his donkey when he saw a troop of men on horseback. Fearing they were robbers, he climbed into a tree. The men dismounted near Ali Baba's hiding place.

Captain: Here we are, men. Let's go quickly inside. Open, Sesame!

Narrator: At that command, a door in the rocks opened up, and the men went inside. Once everyone was inside, the captain called out, "Close, Sesame," and the door closed.

Ali Baba: This must be a magical place. I must find the courage to open the door and go inside!

Narrator: Ali Baba climbed down from the tree and stood in front of the door.

Ali Baba: Open, Sesame!

Narrator: Ali Baba was surprised to find a large, well-lighted vault, with riches all around. Silk, brocade, gold, silver, and leather purses tempted him. He took all he could load onto his donkey and then commanded the door to close. He quickly led the donkey home to his wife.

Ali Baba: Dear wife, look what I have discovered. There is a cave with all sorts of riches inside. This is just a sampling of what remains hidden there, but we mustn't tell anyone. I am going to bury the gold.

Ali Baba's Wife: Let me measure the gold first. While you dig the hole, I will borrow a measure.

Narrator: She ran to borrow the measure from Cassim's wife. Now, Cassim's wife wondered what a poor woman would need with a measure. She cleverly placed a bit of suet in the measure. As Ali Baba's wife measured out the gold, she didn't realize that a bit of it stuck to the suet. When she returned it, Cassim's wife noticed the gold and spoke to her husband.

Cassim's Wife: Cassim, Ali Baba is so rich that he doesn't count his money. He measures it.

Cassim: How can this be? He has never been a man of wealth.

Cassim's Wife: His wife borrowed a measure, and this gold was still in it.

Narrator: Cassim decided to confront Ali Baba and went to his home.

Cassim: Ali Baba, you pretend to be poor. Yet you measure out gold.

Ali Baba: Ah, you have discovered the secret cave. I will share our riches with you if you will keep this just between us.

Cassim: I will keep the secret, but you must show me where to find the treasure. If you don't, you risk losing all of it.

Narrator: When Ali Baba told him where the cave was, Cassim took ten mules to the cave, hoping to get the treasure for himself. Soon he came to the cave.

Cassim: Open, Sesame!

Narrator: The door in the cave opened and shut behind him. Cassim gathered up as many treasures as he could, but when it was time to start loading up the mules, all he could think about was his wealth. He couldn't remember how to open the door again.

Cassim: Open, Barley! Open, Wheat!

Narrator: Cassim kept trying different grains, but couldn't recall the right one. Soon the robbers returned to their cave. They saw the mules and suspected someone had discovered their treasure.

Captain: Open, Sesame!

Narrator: Cassim had heard the robbers' horses and knew that he was in trouble. He threw himself at the captain, but he was quickly overpowered and killed.

Captain: Cut up his body! Nail it to the walls! That will warn other would-be thieves to leave our treasures alone.

Narrator: As night drew on, Cassim's wife grew very uneasy and ran to Ali Baba to tell him where Cassim had gone. Ali comforted her and then set out for the cave. When he saw his dead brother in the cave, he put the body on one of his mules, placing gold on other mules. When he got to Cassim's home, the servant Morgiana opened the door.

Ali Baba: Morgiana, this is the body of your master. He has been murdered, but we must bury him as though he died in his bed. We'll talk more later, but meanwhile call your mistress.

Narrator: While Ali Baba comforted the widow, Morgiana went to see an apothecary.

Morgiana: My poor master, Cassim, can neither eat nor speak. No one knows what is wrong. Do you have some lozenges that might help?

Apothecary: Take these lozenges. They should help ease his pain.

Narrator: She took the lozenges home, but returned the next day to the apothecary. She asked for an essence given only to those who were dying.

Apothecary: I am sorry to hear that Cassim is not doing better. Perhaps he will recover, but this doesn't sound promising.

Narrator: Indeed, no one was surprised to learn soon thereafter that Cassim had died. Morgiana went to see a cobbler next and gave him some gold. She blindfolded him and took him to Cassim's body, which she had the cobbler sew together. After leading the cobbler home, she took the blindfold from his eyes. Soon Cassim was buried. Cassim's widow and Morgiana went to live with Ali Baba. The forty thieves returned to the cave and were astonished to find the body gone along with more of their gold.

Captain: Our treasure trove is surely at risk! We must discover who knows our secret. We've killed one and now we must find the other. I need a bold volunteer who will disguise himself as a traveler and find out who might have been recently buried.

Narrator: One brave thief offered to try. He went into town and began to ask discreet questions. Soon he came to the cobbler's stall.

Thief: Good morning, sir. Tell me, how can an old man such as you still see to stitch shoes?

Cobbler: I may be old, but I still have very good eyes. In fact, I recently sewed together a dead body in less light than I have now.

Thief: Is that right? Well, there's a gold piece in it for you if you can show me where you did this amazing feat.

Cobbler: I can't tell you, sir. I was blindfolded.

Thief: Perhaps another piece of gold will refresh your memory. I suspect you can remember the route you took with a little effort.

Cobbler: Well, perhaps you are right. Why don't you blindfold me as before and I'll see if I can retrace my steps.

Narrator: The cobbler remembered the turns and happily collected his coins. The thief made a chalk mark on the door of Cassim's house and returned to the forest. Later, Morgiana noticed the mark on the door while on an errand. She took a piece of chalk and made the same mark on two or three houses on either side. Meanwhile, the thief had returned to the cave.

Thief: I have found the house where a cobbler sewed up a body. I've marked it with chalk, so we will be able to find it easily.

Narrator: But when the thieves got to the house, the many marks confounded the captain. He immediately ordered that the man be beheaded for his failure. Another thief was sent to have the cobbler show him the house, but Morgiana once again outwitted them with more chalk marks. This thief was also put to death. Then the captain decided to see the cobbler himself. But instead of marking the house, he committed it to memory. He returned to his men.

Captain: Here is my plan. Go to the neighboring villages and buy nineteen mules. Then buy thirty-eight leather jars and place them on the mules. Fill one with oil. Use the others to hide in, one man to each jar. I will seal the jars. Take your weapons and be prepared.

Narrator: The captain, disguised as an oil merchant, led the mules to town, stopping in front of Ali Baba's house. Ali Baba was sitting outside in the cool air.

Captain: I have brought oil from a great distance to sell at tomorrow's market. But it has grown so late that I don't know where to spend the night. Could you take me in?

Narrator: Ali Baba took in the captain and asked Morgiana to fetch him some dinner. Later, the captain slipped outside and quietly instructed each man on what to do.

Captain: When I throw some stones from my bed chamber, cut the jars open with your knives and come out. I will then join you.

Narrator: Later, Morgiana decided to take a bit of oil for her cooking. When she got to a jar, one of the thieves asked her if it was time yet. Once again, she thought quickly, telling the man that it wasn't quite time. She went to each jar, repeating her message. She realized that thirty-eight robbers were about to be let into the house. She went to the jar of oil and filled a large kettle. After boiling the oil, she poured some in every jar, killing each robber inside. Then she went back to the kitchen to see what would happen. Soon the captain awoke. He threw down the pebbles, but when nothing happened, he went outside.

Captain: Are you awake? It's time. Get up! Don't waste any more time.

Narrator: Finally, he realized that all his robbers were dead. He quickly slipped away over the garden wall. The next morning, Ali Baba awoke, and seeing that his guest was gone, spoke to Morgiana.

Ali Baba: What has happened to the oil merchant?

Morgiana: Look in the jars, master.

Narrator: Ali Baba saw the dead men and Morgiana explained what had happened. She told Ali Baba that they were most assuredly the robbers from the forest.

Ali Baba: You have been a good and clever servant. I am going to reward you with your freedom.

Narrator: Ali Baba and Morgiana buried the dead men. They sold the mules in the market. Meanwhile, the captain brooded in the cave where he vowed to get his revenge on Ali Baba. But that's a story for another time, another night.

Grateful Hans

Germany

Summary

In this adaptation of a Brothers Grimm fairy tale, a young man named Hans makes several trades as he travels home to see his mother. Soon he has nothing to show for his seven years of hard work. Despite his losses, Hans finds something to be grateful for at every stage.

Presentation Suggestions

Hans and the narrator have important roles and should practice their lines until they are comfortable. They should have prominent places onstage, standing slightly to one side of the stage. The other characters can enter the stage, read their parts, and then exit after their lines, or they can sit on stools, standing to read their lines.

Props

Each of the characters should dress in simple costumes to suit their roles. The stage could have a backdrop mural of a countryside.

Delivery Suggestions

The spoken parts are somewhat old-fashioned in nature, typical of a fairy tale of the 1800s.

Characters

Narrator
Hans
Master
Horseman
Farmer's Wife
Butcher
Young Woman
Scissors Grinder

Grateful Hans

Narrator: Hans had been an apprentice for seven years, and now that his service was finished, he anxiously prepared to go home.

Hans: Master, my time is up, and I want to go home to see my mother. Would you please give me the wages I have earned during these past seven years?

Master: Hans, you have been a good and faithful worker, and I am going to reward you for your hard work. I hope you'll use what you have learned to your advantage and live a happy life.

Narrator: The master was a generous man, and he considered Hans a good friend. The master gave Hans a lump of gold as big as his head!

Master: Hans, take this gold and use it to establish your new life. Please give your best to your mother and tell her how much I have appreciated your dedication and hard work these past seven years.

Narrator: Hans thanked his master, wrapped his gold in a blanket, and hoisted it onto his shoulder. He walked slowly down the road, trying to find a comfortable way to carry his heavy load. Soon he saw a horseman, riding along comfortably and quickly.

Horseman: Good morning, young man. That's quite a load you're carrying.

Hans: Yes, sir, it does weigh me down. I envy your good fortune with owning such a magnificent horse. It must be a great luxury to be able to ride. How fast you must travel!

Horseman: Why don't you ride a horse, young man?

Hans: I would if I could, but I have this big lump of gold to take home. It's so heavy that I have to carry it on my shoulder, and I can't even hold my head straight.

Horseman: I'll tell you what, young man. I'll trade my horse for that lump of gold. You can travel in ease and go as fast as you want just by saying "Giddyap!"

Hans: What a fine idea, sir, but I must warn you that this is a very heavy lump of gold.

Narrator: The horseman and Hans completed their trade, and Hans rode off, enjoying the breeze and comfort. After a while he decided he wanted to go faster and shouted, "Giddyap!" The horse began to trot briskly, and before Hans knew it, he was thrown into a ditch.

Hans: This is a fine fix I'm in! Why did I ever trade my hard-earned gold for this dangerous, willful horse?

Narrator: As Hans was dusting himself off, a farmer's wife who was leading a cow walked by.

Farmer's Wife: Are you all right, young man? It looks as though that horse threw you a long ways!

Hans: I'm not hurt, but I don't ever want to ride that beastly animal again! I could have broken my neck! Now your cow is quite a different story. You can walk along with her as slowly as you please, plus you are sure to have milk, butter, and cheese every day. I would love to have a fine cow such as yours!

Farmer's Wife: Well, sir, I think we can work that out to both our satisfaction. I would gladly trade you my cow for that horse if it would make you happy.

Hans: That is so very kind of you, and I will gladly accept your offer.

Narrator: Hans walked along with his cow, thinking how grateful he was for his clever trade.

Hans: With this cow and some bread I will never be hungry or thirsty again.

Narrator: That night, Hans used the last of his coins to eat and sleep at an inn. The next morning, he resumed his journey, and because it was a hot day, he decided to stop and milk the cow. He put his leather cap underneath her to catch the milk, but no matter how hard he tried, he had no success in squeezing one drop of milk from her. Finally, the cow got so annoyed with Hans that she kicked him in the head! Just then a butcher came along, carrying a young pig in a wheelbarrow.

Butcher: Say, young man, you look as though you have just been beaten up!

Hans: This miserable cow refuses to give any milk and kicked me in the head for my efforts!

Butcher: That cow is too old to give you any milk. All she is good for is to pull a plow or provide a few dinners.

Hans: Well, that doesn't help me much. I don't have a plow and I don't especially like cow meat! I'd much rather eat pork chops or sausages.

Butcher: Well, young man, I can do you a favor and take that cow off your hands if you would like to take this pig in exchange.

Narrator: The butcher took the pig out of the wheelbarrow, tied a rope to its head, and handed the rope to Hans. Hans thanked him for his kindness and set off down the road again.

Hans: I have so much to be grateful for. Every time I get into a bit of trouble, something happens to straighten it all out again.

Narrator: Soon Hans found himself walking alongside a young woman carrying a fine white goose under her arm. They began to talk with each other as they walked along the road.

Young Woman: That is a fine pig you are leading.

Hans: Yes, I am one fortunate young man. I started out with a heavy lump of gold and traded it for a fine horse. But when that horse turned out to be a problem I was lucky enough to exchange it for a cow. Now that cow turned out to be too old to milk, but a butcher gave me this fine pig in trade. It should provide my mother and me with several delicious dinners.

Young Woman: That is an amazing story, but this goose has been fattened up for eight weeks and will make a wonderful feast for any table. Just lift it, and you'll see what I mean.

Hans: Yes, it is surely a heavy bird, but look at how fine this pig is!

Young Woman: I wonder about that pig, though. You see, I just came through that village, and the mayor had a pig stolen out of his barn. Some men are searching for it, and I hope you didn't trade your cow for a stolen pig!

Hans: Now, how am I going to get out of this fix? I just want to get home! What next?

Young Woman: Perhaps I can help you. I know my way around here and could hide that pig from the men. I'll trade you for it and you won't have to worry about getting caught.

Narrator: Hans gladly made the trade and hurried toward home. On his way through the last village, he saw a scissors grinder hard at work and stopped to watch him for a while.

Hans: What a lucky man you are! Sharpening knives and scissors is a useful trade.

Scissors Grinder: That's true, but you have a fine possession yourself. That's as fat a goose as I have ever seen. Of course, if you knew how to grind scissors you would always have money in your pocket to buy whatever you needed.

Hans: But I don't have a grindstone and can't sharpen anything without one.

Scissors Grinder: Well, I have an extra one that you can have in exchange for that goose.

Narrator: Once again Hans made the trade, thinking about all the money he could make. He took the grindstone and continued down the road, but soon he began to feel hungry and thirsty. The weight of the stone wore him down, and he wished that he didn't have to carry it. Finally, he came to a well, where he decided to rest and have a refreshing drink of water. He laid his grindstone on the edge of the well to keep it safe, but as he leaned over to pull up the bucket, he knocked the grindstone into the well.

From *Multicultural Folktales: Readers Theatre for Elementary Students.* © 2000 Suzanne I. Barchers. Teacher Ideas Press. 1-800-237-6124.

Hans: What a lucky man I am! Now I don't have to carry that heavy grindstone home!

Narrator: Hans got his drink and finished his journey home, grateful for his good fortune for the rest of his days.

The Learned Servant Girl

China

Summary

When a warring lord threatens the peaceful life of the Lord of Luchow's territory, Red Cord, a faithful servant, uses her intelligence and magic to help. She tricks the warring lord into thinking that her lord could have easily killed him. The warring lord professes his devotion to Red Cord's lord, and war is averted.

Presentation Suggestions

The narrator has an important role and should rehearse the script carefully. Because this is a short script, all the characters should stay onstage throughout the script.

Props

Red Cord could wear dark clothes, with a red cord around her waist. The stage could be decorated with Chinese articles, such as vases or artwork. An urn could be placed on the stage.

Delivery Suggestions

The characters can speak in normal voices appropriate for their roles.

Characters

Narrator
Red Cord
Lord of Luchow
Drummer
Messenger
Lord of Weipu

From *Multicultural Folktales: Readers Theatre for Elementary Students.* © 2000 Suzanne I. Barchers. Teacher Ideas Press. 1-800-237-6124.

The Learned Servant Girl

Narrator: During the difficult days of the T'ang Dynasty there was an old lord who governed six districts. The Lord of Luchow had a large household and many servants, but one servant, Red Cord, was a most unusual girl. She had learned to read and she enjoyed reading classic literature. She also played the lute and was skilled in all sorts of the arts. One night, the lord held an elaborate feast. During the feast, Red Cord listened to the far-off drumbeats of a kettledrum and went to the lord out of concern for what she was hearing.

Red Cord: My lord, I believe the drumbeats have an edge of sadness. There seems to be something troubling the drummer.

Narrator: The lord sent for the drummer and talked with him.

Lord of Luchow: Tell me, young man, is there something troubling you?

Drummer: My lord, my wife has just died, and I want to return to my homeland for her burial. But I know it is an imposition to ask such a favor.

Lord of Luchow: Of course you may go, and please accept my condolences on your loss.

Narrator: The young man left to begin his journey home. Meanwhile, a messenger came to see the Lord of Luchow.

Messenger: My lord, I have just learned that the Lord of Weipu plans to overthrow your territory. He has gathered a strong army, has set up camp nearby, and is training the army in the martial arts.

Lord of Luchow: This is valuable information. You know how much I dislike war, and I will have to consider carefully what to do about this threat.

Narrator: Red Cord overheard the conversation and decided to help her lord. She put on dark clothes and slippers and retrieved from her chest a magic sword. She murmured a few magic words and was soon moving away on the wind. She flew through the black night until she could see the dying embers of the enemy's evening campfire. She hovered over the sentries, noting that they drowsed in the heavy night air. She let the wind set her on the ground and sneaked past the sentries to the tent of the Lord of Weipu.

Red Cord: Look at how soundly he sleeps. He makes it easy for me to take that golden urn.

Narrator: Holding the urn and the magic sword, she slipped out of the tent and drifted noiselessly past the guards. She murmured her magic words and flew back to the Lord of Luchow's camp. She went straight to his tent, where she found him unable to sleep.

From *Multicultural Folktales: Readers Theatre for Elementary Students.* © 2000 Suzanne I. Barchers. Teacher Ideas Press. 1-800-237-6124.

Red Cord: My lord, I just returned from the enemy's camp where I stole this golden urn. Return it to the Lord of Weipu by messenger tomorrow and I guarantee that he will no longer threaten you.

Lord of Luchow: I am not sure that I understand your purpose, but I haven't any better ideas.

Narrator: The next day, the Lord of Luchow sent his faithful messenger to the enemy's camp.

Messenger: I have come to give this urn to the Lord of Weipu.

Narrator: The Lord of Weipu accepted the urn and sent the messenger back to his home. Then he thought about what receiving the urn could mean.

Lord of Weipu: This is quite disturbing. If the Lord of Luchow could take this urn from my tent, he could just as easily take my life. It seems that I have no choice but to write to him with my thanks for returning the urn and for sparing my life.

Narrator: The Lord of Weipu sent his thanks and also pledged his devotion to the Lord of Luchow. After reading the message, the Lord of Luchow sent for Red Cord.

Lord of Luchow: Red Cord, I see now what you planned. The Lord of Weipu has pledged himself to me. Thanks to you we have been spared war.

Narrator: Red Cord and the lord celebrated Red Cord's cleverness, and they enjoyed a long and prosperous time of peace.

Legend of the Feathered Serpent

Mexico

Summary

In this Aztec legend, Moctezuma realizes that his rule is ending. He prepares for the new god to arrive, but when the new god comes, he is not the powerful Feathered Serpent they expect. Instead, he is a cruel, greedy, bearded one. The invaders destroy much of what the people love and honor, until finally they take a stand, saving their beloved god of flowers and arts.

Presentation Suggestions

The narrator and Moctezuma have long roles and should have prominent positions. Moctezuma can stand next to the narrator, with the other characters standing on his other side. If desired, designate two narrators.

Props

If possible, find examples of Aztec art. Consider making a mural of the Aztec calendar. The characters could dress in bright, colorful clothing. Statues could be added to the stage.

Delivery Suggestions

The narrator has a long script and should carefully rehearse the many difficult words. Moctezuma should sound proud, yet resigned to his fate. The priest, nobleman, wizard, man, and Itauqui should sound normal, varying the intensity of their reading according to the plot.

Characters

Narrator

Priest

Nobleman

Wizard

Moctezuma

Man

Itauqui

"Legend of the Feathered Serpent" is adapted from "Legend of the Feathered Serpent: An Aztec Legend" in *The Eagle and the Rainbow: Timeless Tales from México* by Antonio Hernández Madrigal, illustrated by Tomie dePaola (Golden, CO: Fulcrum, 1997), 43–53. Used with permission.

Legend of the Feathered Serpent

Narrator: The year One Reed was near, and Quetzalcóatal, the Feathered Serpent, God of Life and Learning, had promised to return and reclaim his power and his people. Everyone lived in fear, but Moctezuma knew the most fear. He lived in a palace as large as a city, and his palace was surrounded by forests and beautiful gardens. While he rested in his favorite courtyard, his servants would offer him many different dishes. But he no longer felt pleasure as the prophecy haunted his long days and sleepless nights. One day, a priest, a nobleman, and a wizard came to see him.

Priest: Great Lord, strange signs and omens are appearing on earth and in the sky.

Nobleman: The people wake at night from the strange howls and cries.

Wizard: Our nights are plagued with horrible dreams and visions.

Moctezuma: Do not be afraid. You must remember that all that begins also comes to an end. I, the ruler of this great empire, shall guide my people in the last days.

Narrator: Moctezuma stayed alone in his sleeping chamber. He used sharp needles from the agave cactus to pierce his body in sacrifice to the gods. He did not eat or drink, fasting to purify himself. Many days later, he sent for his helpers.

Moctezuma: We must prepare to welcome the Feathered Serpent who will soon take my place.

Narrator: The next morning, the people were awakened by a call from conch shells. They came to the palace where Moctezuma addressed them.

Moctezuma: He who left to the east is coming back. And after the great Feathered Serpent returns, I shall no longer rule.

Man: Will he be angry with us and our children? Will he take revenge on us?

Moctezuma: The Feathered Serpent must be loved and respected. We shall obey his ways and avoid all that may displease him or provoke his wrath.

Narrator: As the year One Reed began, Moctezuma became more and more anxious. One morning, his servant came to him. The servant told Moctezuma that one of the guards by the water saw floating rafts as big as houses coming over the waters. Moctezuma called for his noblemen.

Moctezuma: The time has come. We must find an offering worthy for the mighty Feathered Serpent. Let all the workers prepare fine jewels and clothes.

Narrator: Finally, Moctezuma traveled to meet the bearded god. He laid his offerings at the god's feet. The god smiled at the gifts. When Moctezuma pledged his support, the bearded one didn't understand the strange language. But he knew the gifts were fine and went with Moctezuma back to the palace. At first, the bearded god and his men were happy, but soon they began to demand more and more. The people complained to Moctezuma.

Man: Why do you allow the bearded men to be so unkind?

Moctezuma: We should not anger them. We should try to please and obey them.

Man: Are you no longer our ruler?

Moctezuma: Quetzalcóatal now sits at my throne. He is our new lord and ruler.

Narrator: The people were disappointed when they realized that Moctezuma saw the bearded man as the long-awaited god. The evil men became more bold. They destroyed the temples and stole gold and jewels from the people. They tortured anyone who stood in their way. Soon much of the city was destroyed. The people realized that the bearded one was not a true god. The priest brought sad news to the people.

Priest: Our lord Moctezuma has been killed by the invaders. We can't trust them. We should defend ourselves.

Nobleman: But how can we fight them?

Itauqui: Even Xochipilli, our god of flowers and arts, is at risk.

Priest: We should try to save his temple at all costs. Itauqui, you should continue to guard the temple, and we will try to help you.

Narrator: Soon the evil men came to the temple of Xochipilli. They saw the jewels on the god and tried to remove them. But they couldn't get any jewels off. They encircled the statue and tried to lift it, but it was too heavy. Finally, they wrapped ropes around the statue and began to drag it away. The priest ran to raise the alarm.

Priest: They are stealing the Xochipilli!

Nobleman: How will we make our music and dance without this god?

Wizard: We need to go after them.

Narrator: Many people joined together. They waited until dark when the invaders were sleeping by the fire. They took the ropes and began to pull the statue back to the temple. Just as they neared the temple, they heard the pounding of hooves of the horses.

Itauqui: They are coming! How can we save Xochipilli?

Wizard: Let's dig a hiding place for Xochipilli. We'll bury him.

Narrator: They all worked quickly, running away when they were done. Itauqui began to walk toward the village. The men appeared, and they noticed that Itauqui's hands were blistered and bleeding. They lashed at him, demanding to know where the statue was. But Itauqui stayed quiet. Finally, they realized they would learn nothing from him. They tied him up, built a fire, and placed his feet on the burning embers. But Itauqui never cried out. Finally, he died with a peaceful smile on his face.

    The next day the invaders left. The villagers returned to where they had buried Xochipilli. They found Itauqui's body on the ground. They sadly carried both back to the temple. They dug a grave for Itauqui and then returned Xochipilli to his god's place of honor. Itauqui became known as the courageous protector of Xochipilli. His name and courage live forever in the hearts of the Aztec people.

The Magic Fan

India

Summary

When Imani tells her father that she wants to be independent, he sends her to live with a religious man. Through her hard work, Imani achieves success. While traveling, her father acquires a box with a magic fan. The fan brings a king to Imani's home and they all become good friends. Imani's jealous sister poisons the king, and Imani has to travel in disguise to her friend's kingdom, where she heals the king. Finally, the king returns to her and realizes that she saved him.

Presentation Suggestions

The narrator reads frequently throughout the story and should be placed prominently on the stage. The two monkeys can enter for their lines and then leave. Imani, the fakir, and King Subbar Khan should have prominent placement.

Props

A spinning wheel or loom would make a dramatic addition to the setting. Decorate the stage with Oriental fans or create a mural using fans as the motif. Draped pieces of brilliant cloth would also provide an interesting focal point.

Delivery Suggestions

The characters with long roles should carefully rehearse their parts to ensure smooth delivery. No special voices are needed, except perhaps for the monkeys.

Characters

Narrator
King
Kupti
Imani
Fakir
Servant
King Subbar Khan
First Monkey
Second Monkey

From *Multicultural Folktales: Readers Theatre for Elementary Students.* © 2000 Suzanne I. Barchers. Teacher Ideas Press. 1-800-237-6124.

The Magic Fan

Narrator: A king dearly loved his two daughters, Kupti and Imani. One day, he asked each of his daughters an important question.

King: Kupti, are you content to have me manage your life and your wealth?

Kupti: Of course, dear Father, I trust you with everything.

King: Imani, are you content to have me manage your life and your wealth?

Imani: Father, though I love you dearly, I would rather be in charge of my own life and fortune.

King: I fear you are young and foolish, but I shall grant you your wish. I will arrange it so that you can learn the meaning of independence.

Narrator: The king presented Imani to an old, lame fakir, who was a religious man. The king told the fakir that Imani would be staying with him and earning her living. The fakir was amazed by this event, but he had no choice in the matter. Because his home was quite humble, he puzzled over how he could make Imani comfortable. Imani had her own ideas, though.

Imani: Do you have any money?

Fakir: I have only one penny.

Imani: That will be enough. Give it to me and then borrow a spinning wheel and loom for me.

Narrator: While the fakir went to borrow the spinning wheel and loom, the princess took the penny and bought flax and oil. When she returned, she used the oil to soothe the fakir's lame leg and then began to work at the spinning wheel.

Fakir: Your thread is beautiful! What are you going to do with it?

Imani: If you think the thread is beautiful, watch what I make with it. The cloth will be even better.

Narrator: The cloth was indeed breathtaking. She sent the fakir to the market to sell the cloth, and while he was at the market, Kupti came by to shop.

Kupti: How much is that remarkable piece of cloth?

Fakir: The price is two gold pieces.

Kupti: I will buy it! What a wonderful piece of cloth!

From *Multicultural Folktales: Readers Theatre for Elementary Students.* © 2000 Suzanne I. Barchers. Teacher Ideas Press. 1-800-237-6124.

Narrator: Kupti was delighted with her purchase. Each day, Imani sent the fakir to the market with a penny. He would buy flax and oil. Each day, she would rub oil into his crooked leg and weave her lovely cloth. The fakir's leg slowly improved, and her cloth sold for handsome prices.

Imani: My friend, I think it is time we enjoy our success. Let's build a fine home.

Fakir: Your spinning has made us rich, far richer than I thought I would ever be.

Narrator: They built their house, and the king was pleased by their success. Soon the king had to travel to another country, but before he left, he called for Kupti.

King: Kupti, I will be gone for some time. What would you like for a gift when I return?

Kupti: I would dearly love a necklace of rubies.

Narrator: The king sent a servant to Imani with the same request. When the servant got there, Imani was busy trying to untangle a knot of thread in her loom.

Servant: The king is taking an extended journey. He asks what you would like as a gift.

Narrator: Imani was so absorbed in her task that she didn't pay much attention to his question.

Imani: Patience, patience.

Narrator: The servant assumed that was Imani's answer and returned to the king.

King: What gift would Imani like?

Servant: She asked for only one thing, Your Majesty. Patience.

King: That is a strange request. I'm not sure how I'll be able to fulfill it.

Narrator: The king went on his trip. As he neared the end of his travels, he purchased the necklace for Kupti, but he still had not found patience for Imani. He sent his servant to the marketplace to ask if anyone had patience to sell. The servant felt foolish, but he followed the king's order as he strolled through the marketplace.

Servant: Does anyone have patience for sale? Any patience for sale?

Narrator: The king of this country heard about the servant's strange request and sent for him.

King Subbar Khan: Why are you asking for patience?

Servant: My master wants it as a present for his daughter.

King Subbar Khan: Well, the only patience this lady may have cannot be bought.

From *Multicultural Folktales: Readers Theatre for Elementary Students.* © 2000 Suzanne I. Barchers. Teacher Ideas Press. 1-800-237-6124.

Servant: Well, Your Majesty, I don't know why the princess even wants patience. She is not only beautiful and clever, but she also works hard and shows great love.

Narrator: The king left for a moment, returning with a fan that he put in a small box.

King Subbar Khan: Here is a box. It will open only for the person who needs its contents. The person who opens it will receive patience of one sort or another.

Narrator: The servant took it to his master and they returned home. When Imani received the box, she was surprised because she had not expected a gift. She gave it to the fakir, but without a key or hinge he could not open it. But when Imani took it back and held it, the box opened quite easily. Imani took out the fan and began to use it. With the third stroke of the fan, the foreign king suddenly stood before her.

King Subbar Khan: I am King Subbar Khan. A servant came to the marketplace in my country, looking for patience, so I gave him this box and fan. The box will not open to just anyone, but when it does open, the magic is powerful. Just three strokes of the fan will bring me here, and three taps of the fan will send me home again.

Narrator: The king stayed for the evening, enjoying the company of Imani and the fakir. The fakir and the king enjoyed many hours of conversation, playing chess together late into the night. Imani set up a room for the king to sleep in when he stayed late, and then she would send him home in the morning.

Kupti soon learned that a handsome king was visiting her sister, and she began to feel very jealous. She decided to pay Imani a visit to see what she could learn. After discovering which was the king's room, she sneaked into it and spread finely ground, poisoned glass on the bed.

After that night's chess game, the king retired to his bed. When he lay down, the glass began to prick him. He suspected he had been poisoned, but the next morning, he showed no signs of his distress and returned home as usual. He became weak from the poison and lay near death. None of his physicians could help him. Meanwhile, Imani wondered what had happened to their friend.

Imani: My fan doesn't work anymore. No matter how much I try, the king doesn't come back to us. What shall we do?

Fakir: I see no solution except for one of us to go to his kingdom and try to discover what has happened.

Narrator: Imani decided to dress like a young fakir and travel alone to his country. She lay down under a tree to sleep, but thoughts of the king kept her awake. As she lay there, two monkeys chattered in the tree above her.

First Monkey: I have heard that the king is dying.

From *Multicultural Folktales: Readers Theatre for Elementary Students.* © 2000 Suzanne I. Barchers. Teacher Ideas Press. 1-800-237-6124.

Second Monkey: Yes, I heard that some poisoned glass was put in his bed.

First Monkey: It's too bad that no one knows how to heal him.

Second Monkey: It's really quite simple. Just soaking the berries from this very tree in hot water will provide the cure he needs. The king would soon recover.

Narrator: The next morning, Imani gathered all the berries she could carry. She went to the palace and told the servants that she had a cure for the king. When she saw the king, she could hardly recognize him. She spoke to the servant.

Imani: Bring me some boiling water. After I prepare this potion, have his attendant wash him with it. Do this every day.

Narrator: Gradually, the king began to feel better. After the second washing, he asked for some broth. After the third washing, he sat up. After the fourth washing, he went to his throne and asked to see the physician who had cured him. When Imani was brought before him, she was still in her disguise, and the king didn't recognize her.

King Subbar Khan: Thank you for all you have done for me. How can I reward you? Ask for anything and it will be yours.

Imani: All I ask is to receive your ring and handkerchief.

Narrator: Imani received his ring and handkerchief and returned to her home. Then she sent for the king with her magic fan.

Imani: We have missed you, dear friend. Why didn't you come to us for so long?

King Subbar Khan: I was taken ill and nearly died. But a remarkable physician came and healed me. All he wanted was my ring and handkerchief in reward.

Imani: Are these the ring and handkerchief?

Narrator: The king realized that Imani was truly the physician. He suddenly took the magic fan from her.

King Subbar Khan: Imani, I will never go back to my country unless you accompany me as my wife!

Narrator: And so it was that the fakir returned with Imani and the king to the king's country where they celebrated the marriage and lived happily ever after.

Princess Maya

India

Summary

A king has twin daughters. He decides to marry one of them to the first man he sees one morning. The man appears to be a beggar, but he really travels as a beggar because a snake has taken over his body. Princess Maya uses her wit to kill the snake, freeing her new husband from continuing misery.

Presentation Suggestions

Maya should be in the center of the stage. The king should be to one side of her with the groom on the other side. The counselor should be on the other side of the king with the narrator next to the counselor. The first snake and second snake can stand on the other side of the groom.

Props

Toy snakes could be placed onstage. A mural could be created that shows a rural scene with a castle on one side. The king and Maya could be dressed in royal colors, with the groom dressed like a beggar.

Delivery Suggestions

Maya should sound wise and thoughtful. The king should sound exasperated with some of Maya's responses. The groom should sound desperate when describing his problems with eating.

Characters

Narrator
King
Maya
Counselor
Groom
First Snake
Second Snake

Princess Maya

Narrator: There was an old king whose wife had died. He was no longer wealthy, but he took great joy in his twin daughters, Madri and Maya. Although they were equally beautiful, they didn't have the same temperament. Madri was content to stay at home, chatting with her friends about things of the court. Maya loved to travel and study, an unusual pastime for a princess. She especially loved to learn the language of the animals. One morning, her father greeted her in his usual fashion.

King: Good morning, Maya.

Maya: Good morning, dear Father. Your deserts!

King: What kind of greeting is that? Your deserts? Hmm.

Narrator: Another day, he lost his temper when Maya's laughter woke him from his nap.

King: Can't a man sleep in peace? Or was it my snores that amused you?

Maya: I didn't laugh at your snores, Father.

King: What was it then?

Maya: I overheard two ants speaking as they crawled on your couch.

King: Now tell me, what did those ants have to say?

Maya: I'd rather not say, Father.

King: I want you to tell me. Now, Maya.

Maya: Well, they were talking about how both of them had no suitors for their daughters. They were hoping that you would give a wedding banquet for one of your daughters. Then they might find grooms for *their* daughters.

King: That is hardly amusing, Maya.

Maya: Father, what made me laugh is that one of them wondered how the king could sleep in peace with two unmarried daughters under his roof.

King: Hmmm. I'm afraid I don't share your amusement, Maya.

Narrator: But the king thought about what Maya had said. The next morning, he called his chief counselor to him.

King: I'm beginning to think there's something wrong with Maya. What do you think?

Counselor: If the queen were alive, she could have explained it to you. You see, your daughters are old enough to marry. They are no longer children.

King: Without dowries though, marriage will be difficult. Anyway, I don't understand why Maya is so different from Madri. They are identical twins, yet Maya is so independent. Why can't she be like Madri?

Counselor: I think Maya is an intelligent young woman. She would benefit from having a husband, even if he were poor.

Narrator: The king pondered this, deciding his advisor was right. The next morning, he called for Maya.

King: Maya, you will have your own deserts today. I decided that the first available man I saw today would become your husband. And the first man I saw was a beggar from Avanti.

Narrator: The king later regretted his impulsive choice, but Maya decided to make the best of it. Indeed, as she left the wedding, she made a cheerful statement.

Maya: Better to have a beggar as spouse than dwell alone in a great king's house!

King: It sounds as though Maya has learned wisdom from her studies. I hope it serves her well.

Narrator: As the beggar and Maya left, her groom told her that he had a story to tell.

Groom: I am not really a beggar. I travel because I am too embarrassed to stay in any one place. You see, one day I fell asleep by an anthill. Ever since that day I have been constantly hungry. Yet food doesn't satisfy me. My father hired many doctors, but nothing helped. I was so ashamed of my greediness that I ran away.

Maya: There must be a cure. We can't give up hope. Give me some time to think about this.

Groom: I hope you can help. I'm exhausted from trying to eat enough and never feeling fed.

Narrator: Maya thought for some time. Then she had a suggestion.

Maya: Let's return to the anthill. Maybe I'll get an idea from being there.

Narrator: When they arrived, Maya's husband looked so tired that she told him to rest. Maya went into town for food while her husband slept under a mango tree. When Maya returned, she saw that the head of a snake was sliding out of her husband's mouth. Another snake was slithering out of the anthill. Maya hid behind a bush and listened to the snakes talk.

From *Multicultural Folktales: Readers Theatre for Elementary Students.* © 2000 Suzanne I. Barchers. Teacher Ideas Press. 1-800-237-6124.

First Snake: You are the lowest form of all creatures. You take all the man's food. He will soon die from starvation and then what will you do?

Second Snake: You should talk! You lie on that anthill keeping others from the treasures below it. Those treasures do you no good, yet you hide them. You are jealous because I am fat from all these feedings.

First Snake: I'm not jealous! Someday someone will realize that a bit of black mustard seed will be the end of you!

Second Snake: And if that happens, I hope you are drowned in a bucket of vinegar!

Narrator: Maya understood all they were saying. She quickly obtained the mustard seed and vinegar and killed the snakes. Her husband was cured, and they retrieved the treasure. They returned to his home, where he resumed his position as a prince. And Maya got her deserts as well as a happy life.

The Seven Pairs of Slippers

Portugal

Summary

A princess wears out seven pairs of iron slippers every night. Her father issues a decree, challenging anyone to discover what she does to wear out the iron slippers. A soldier, who has used his wit to obtain a magic cap and boots, accepts the challenge. He discovers that the princess spends the night dancing with a giant. When the soldier confronts her with the slippers, the princess confesses the truth. The king invites the soldier to stay at the castle, and eventually he and the princess marry.

Presentation Suggestions

The narrator and soldier have the primary roles. The four brothers can leave the stage or sit down after they read.

Props

The soldier can wear tall boots and carry a cap. He can be dressed like a soldier, perhaps with a mock sword in his belt. The brothers can be dressed simply. The king and princess can be dressed in royal clothing. Several pairs of slippers could decorate the stage.

Delivery Suggestions

The soldier should sound trustful so that the brothers easily believe him when he suggests they race to the orange. The king should sound powerful. The princess should sound defiant and then resigned.

Characters

Narrator
Soldier
First Brother
Second Brother
Third Brother
Fourth Brother
King
Princess

The Seven Pairs of Slippers

Narrator: Once there was a king and queen who had a princess. Every evening, she wore out seven pairs of iron slippers. The king was always trying to discover how she did this. Finally, he issued a decree challenging anyone to find out how the princess managed to wear out seven pairs of iron slippers every night. The man who succeeded would be given the princess in marriage. If a woman succeeded, she would be married to a prince. One day, a soldier with a sack of oranges over his shoulder was walking along a country road. He came upon two men fighting.

Soldier: Men, why are you fighting?

First Brother: We are brothers. Our father has died, leaving us this cap, and we both want it.

Soldier: You are fighting over a simple cap?

Second Brother: It isn't just a simple cap. It's magic, and anyone who wears it becomes invisible once he says, "Cap, make me invisible."

Soldier: I'll tell what I'll do. Let me stay here with the cap while I throw this orange as far as I can. The one who runs and gets the orange shall get the cap.

First Brother: That sounds better than fighting.

Second Brother: I agree that it's a fair contest.

Narrator: The soldier threw the orange, and the men both ran to pick it up. The soldier wasted no time putting on the cap.

Soldier: Cap, make me invisible.

Narrator: The men returned and no one was there. The soldier went along the road, taking off the cap after a while. He came to two more men who were fighting.

Soldier: Why are you men fighting?

Third Brother: You are right to ask, but the answer rests in these boots.

Fourth Brother: Our father died and left us these boots, and we both want them.

Soldier: Why would you fight over a simple pair of boots?

Third Brother: Ah, but the boots aren't so simple.

Fourth Brother: That's right, these are magic boots. All you have to do is put them on and say, "Boots, take me there," and off you go in an instant.

From *Multicultural Folktales: Readers Theatre for Elementary Students.* © 2000 Suzanne I. Barchers. Teacher Ideas Press. 1-800-237-6124.

Soldier: Those are indeed fine boots. I have an idea for you, though. I'll watch your boots while I throw one of my oranges as far as I can. Whoever gets to the orange first keeps the boots.

Narrator: The brothers agreed, and once again the soldier threw an orange as far away as he could. While the brothers ran after it, he put on the boots and cap.

Soldier: Cap, make me invisible, and boots take me to the city!

Narrator: The brothers found that the soldier had disappeared when they returned with the orange. Meanwhile, the soldier was in the city, where he eventually heard about the king's decree.

Soldier: Surely with this magic cap and these magic boots I can discover how the princess is wearing out her iron slippers every night.

Narrator: The soldier went to tell the king he wanted to accept the challenge.

King: Are you sure you want to try this? Do you really know a way to find out how my daughter is wearing out seven pairs of iron slippers every night?

Solider: Your Majesty, I ask only that you let me try.

King: All right, you can stay in the palace for the next few days. You'll eat with us and sleep in my daughter's room so that you can watch her every move.

Narrator: The first night, the princess gave the soldier a hot drink at bedtime. He didn't realize that she had put a sleeping potion in it, and he fell asleep so soundly that he saw nothing. The next morning, he sat down to breakfast with the king.

King: So what did you discover last night?

Soldier: I'm afraid I saw nothing, Your Majesty.

King: Well, I hope you do better tonight. I'll give you two more nights, but if you fail you will die.

Narrator: That night, the princess gave the soldier another hot drink, and he slept soundly through the night. The next morning, he had to confess to the king that he saw nothing.

King: Well, this is your last chance. If you fail tonight, you will die tomorrow.

Narrator: The soldier began to think about what had happened and decided he would only pretend to drink from the cup the princess brought that night. He pretended to fall asleep, and soon he saw her rise up, dress, take a bag with seven pairs of iron slippers, and begin to leave. He put on his cap and boots, and spoke quietly.

Soldier: Cap, make me invisible, and boots, take me wherever the princess goes.

Narrator: The soldier followed the princess as she got into a carriage that took her to the seashore. She boarded a boat, sailing until she came to the land of the giants. She went to a beautiful palace, entered, and went to a dancing hall, where she began to dance with a giant. When they finished, the princess's iron slippers were in pieces. She put them under a chair, and put on a new pair for the next dance. The invisible soldier slipped the tattered pair in his sack. Each time she danced, she wore out the iron slippers. The soldier gathered them all and put them in his sack. When the princess started home, the soldier told his boots to take him home, so that he could appear to be sleeping in her room. The next morning, he went to eat breakfast with the king.

King: Well, soldier, did you see anything last night?

Soldier: Your Majesty, I'm afraid I saw nothing whatever last night.

King: Then you need to be ready to die today.

Soldier: If that is what must be, then I am ready. But I would ask one favor of you first. Could I speak with the princess?

King: I suppose that's a simple enough request to fulfill.

Narrator: The princess had heard that the soldier was to die and had been quite relieved that she hadn't been discovered. When she was summoned, she went to see her father, having no idea of the soldier's request.

Princess: Father, did you need me?

King: Yes, the soldier wishes to speak with you.

Princess: All right, what do you want?

Soldier: Is it true that you went out at midnight last night?

Princess: That is not true.

Soldier: Is it true that you entered a carriage, went on a ship, and then went to a dance in the kingdom of the giants?

Princess: That is not true.

Soldier: Is it true that you tore seven pairs of iron slippers when you danced with the giant seven times?

Princess: There is no truth in anything you say.

Soldier: Is it true that these are the seven pair of slippers that you wore out?

From *Multicultural Folktales: Readers Theatre for Elementary Students.* © 2000 Suzanne I. Barchers. Teacher Ideas Press. 1-800-237-6124.

Narrator: The soldier took the tattered slippers out of the sack, and the princess realized that she had indeed been caught.

Princess: Yes, it is true, those are my slippers.

King: So the soldier has found out what you have been doing!

Princess: Yes, Father, he has discovered the truth.

Narrator: The king was delighted with the soldier's success and invited him to come and live at the castle. After some time, the princess and soldier fell in love and they married. From that day forward, the only slippers she wore out were the cloth ones she wore when she danced with her husband.

The Snow Queen

Denmark

Summary

When the Snow Queen kidnaps Kay, Gerda sets out to rescue him. She has many adventures along the way, but finally finds Kay in the Snow Queen's icy castle. Gerda's tears break the spell that has held Kay captive, and Gerda takes him home to their grandmother. This is an adaptation of a Hans Christian Andersen story.

Presentation Suggestions

Because there is extensive narration, two narrators are indicated. They could stand alongside each other or on opposite sides of the stage. Gerda's role is also lengthy and should be carefully rehearsed. Characters with smaller roles could exit after reading their parts.

Props

Gerda and Kay could be dressed like young children. The Snow Queen could be draped in white blankets or robes. A sled could decorate the stage, with artificial snow placed in piles.

Delivery Suggestions

Most characters should read their parts in voices consistent with the script. The crows could take on raucous, humorous tones. The Snow Queen should sound cold and icy. The old women should sound caring and helpful.

Characters

First Narrator	Crow
Second Narrator	Robber Queen
Grandmother	Robber Girl
Kay	Wood Pigeon
Gerda	Lapland Woman
Snow Queen	Finland Woman
Old Woman	

The Snow Queen

First Narrator: Once there was a dreadfully wicked hobgoblin who was delighted because he had made a special mirror. Everything that was good and beautiful looked small and unimportant, while everything that was bad and ugly stood out and looked much worse. The hobgoblin admired how everything appeared repulsive. But one day, he dropped the mirror and it broke into a million pieces. Unfortunately, the tiny pieces flew about over the world as if they were grains of sand. The tiniest pieces caught in peoples eyes and hearts, making them see everything awry or causing their hearts to turn to ice. The hobgoblin laughed and laughed at the havoc he had caused.

Second Narrator: Meanwhile, in a large nearby town, two poor children who were best friends lived quietly. In the summer they played outside in the rose gardens, but in the winter they looked longingly out the cold and frosty windows. One snowy day, they were visiting with Grandmother.

Grandmother: Look at the snow, children. It's the white bees swarming.

Kay: Do snowflakes have a queen bee also?

Grandmother: To be sure, my dear. She is the Snow Queen, and she flies wherever they swarm the thickest. She is larger than any of them and never stays upon the earth, flying up into the black clouds instead. At midnight she flies through the streets and peeps in at all the windows, freezing them in such pretty patterns, looking just like flowers.

Gerda: I have seen that, Grandmother! Can the Snow Queen come in here?

Kay: Just let her try! I would put her on the stove and melt her!

First Narrator: Grandmother stroked Kay's hair and told them more stories. That evening, when he was going to bed, Kay jumped on the chair by the window and looked through a small hole. A few snowflakes were falling outside, and one large snowflake lay on the edge of the window box. It grew larger and larger until it took on the shape of a tall, slender women, dressed in the finest white clothes.

Second Narrator: She was indeed beautiful, but Kay couldn't tell that she really was made of ice, hard, bright ice. Still, she seemed alive and her eyes glittered like two stars. But there was no rest or peace in her eyes. She looked at Kay and beckoned to him with her hand, but he was frightened and jumped down from the chair.

From *Multicultural Folktales: Readers Theatre for Elementary Students.* © 2000 Suzanne I. Barchers. Teacher Ideas Press. 1-800-237-6124.

First Narrator: The next day, the weather began to get warmer. Spring and then summer came, and the roses grew more beautifully than ever. Kay and Gerda were looking at a picture book when Kay suddenly cried out.

Kay: Gerda, something has just stung my heart, and I have something in my eye!

Second Narrator: Gerda looked carefully, but couldn't see anything in Kay's eye. Sadly, it was one of the splinters from the hateful hobgoblin's mirror. It made everything look ugly to Kay, and his heart immediately became a lump of ice. Gerda looked at her beloved Kay and began to cry.

Kay: Why are you crying? You look ugly when you cry. And look at those roses! Why, that one is covered with slugs and the others are stunted! I'm going to tear them up!

Gerda: Kay, what are you doing? Stop that!

First Narrator: Kay pulled off some of the roses and then ran into his room. When Gerda tried to look at the picture book with him, he declared that picture books were for babies. From that day forward, Kay's games changed and he took delight in teasing Gerda. He would even imitate Grandmother, putting on her spectacles and walking like an old woman.

Second Narrator: On wintry days, Kay would spend his time admiring the snow instead of playing with Gerda. One day, he took his sled and headed out to play with the boys. While he was playing with them, a huge sleigh came into the town. A large white figure drove the sleigh slowly around the square. Kay tied his sled to the sleigh and let it pull him down the street. At times Kay would try to untie his sled, but the driver began to go like the wind and Kay couldn't get loose.

First Narrator: Kay became terribly frightened, but no matter how loud he cried, no one heard him. The snowflakes began to grow larger and larger while they fell faster and faster. Finally, the sleigh pulled up and the driver stood up. It was a tall, slender woman, the Snow Queen.

Snow Queen: We have traveled a long way and you must be frozen. Here, creep in under my cloak.

Kay: But my sled! Don't forget it!

Second Narrator: But the Snow Queen kissed Kay, and he forgot all about his sled, Gerda, Grandmother, and everybody at home.

Snow Queen: I must not kiss you again or you will freeze to death. Let us be off.

From *Multicultural Folktales: Readers Theatre for Elementary Students.* © 2000 Suzanne I. Barchers. Teacher Ideas Press. 1-800-237-6124.

First Narrator: They flew off over forests and lakes, over land and sea. The cold wind whistled around them, the wolves howled, and the snow hissed while crows shrieked overhead. When they arrived at the Snow Queen's castle, Kay passed the long winter nights looking at the moon and the days sleeping at the Snow Queen's feet.

Second Narrator: Meanwhile, Gerda asked everyone if they knew what had happened to Kay. The other boys told how they had seen him fasten his sled to the large sleigh and how he never returned. Gerda cried and cried all winter long. When spring came, she decided she had to go in search of him. She went to the river and found a boat. Climbing in, she hoped that it would take her to Kay. After some time, the river brought her to a house where an old woman lived.

Old Woman: You poor little girl! What brings you here all alone on that boat?

Gerda: I am searching for my friend Kay. He left with someone on a large sleigh last winter and never returned.

Old Woman: Your friend hasn't come this way, but why don't you stay here and wait? Perhaps he'll come soon and you can go home together.

First Narrator: Gerda went with the old woman into her house, which was filled with delicious food. The old woman enjoyed caring for Gerda, combing her hair and feeding her delicacies.

Old Woman: I have always longed to have a dear little girl, and now you see how happy we are together!

Second Narrator: Gerda didn't realize that the old woman truly was a wicked witch. She took Gerda into her garden, encouraging her to play in the blossoms, which seemed to grow all year-round. So many days passed that Gerda almost forgot about Kay. But one day, she spied a rose that reminded her of the rose gardens she and Kay used to play in. She sat down and cried, thinking of her lost friend.

Gerda: What am I doing here? I need to look for Kay!

First Narrator: Gerda ran to the gate, pushed on the rusty lock, and began to run as fast as she could. When she couldn't run any longer, she sat down on a large stone and looked around her.

Gerda: Oh dear, it is already autumn. I have to keep searching for Kay!

Second Narrator: Gerda ran on, getting tired as it grew colder and the snow appeared. When she stopped to rest again, a large crow perched on the snow in front of her.

Crow: Caw! Caw! Good day, young lady. Will you please tell me what brings you out here all by yourself?

From *Multicultural Folktales: Readers Theatre for Elementary Students.* © 2000 Suzanne I. Barchers. Teacher Ideas Press. 1-800-237-6124.

Gerda: I am searching for my best friend, who was led off by a large sleigh during the winter.

Crow: I might be able to help you find him. I think he is the one who will be marrying the princess, but by now he has surely forgotten you. You see, in this kingdom there is a princess who wanted to find a husband who would do exactly as she told him, never speaking up for himself. Indeed, she advertised that the man who came to the palace and spoke the best would become her husband. Men came in streams, but it wasn't until one young man came that the princess told her court ladies that she had finally found the perfect young man. You see, my friend in the castle, a beautiful crow herself, heard the conversation herself.

Gerda: But how do we know that it is Kay?

Crow: Well, the young man who came was dressed poorly, although he had new boots on.

Gerda: Yes, Kay did have new boots that Grandmother had given him.

Crow: I heard from my sweetheart that the young man was merry and quick-witted, but that he had little to say. He told the princess that he hadn't come to court her, but to listen to her wisdom. That is when they fell in love with each other.

Gerda: That sounds like Kay, but can you lead me to the palace?

Crow: Well, I'm not sure that they would ever let a girl like you in the palace, but wait here, and I will fly to my sweetheart and ask her advice.

First Narrator: The crow returned late in the evening.

Crow: You cannot come into the palace because the guards would never allow it, but my sweetheart knows some backstairs that lead to the sleeping room. Let's go, dear.

Second Narrator: The crow led Gerda to the back door, and when all the lights were out, they slipped inside. On the stairs, Gerda met the crow's sweetheart, who led her up to the sleeping room. But when she got there, she found that the young man was not Kay! Her outcry woke the princess, who asked what was happening. Gerda explained and the kindhearted princess took pity on her.

First Narrator: The next day the princess dressed Gerda in warm clothes, fed her, and gave her a fine coach and footmen so that she could continue her search. Gerda started on her way, but before long some robbers spied the coach, killing the footmen and dragging Gerda out.

Robber Queen: What a fine young girl! I think I will kill her and have her for my dinner.

From *Multicultural Folktales: Readers Theatre for Elementary Students*. © 2000 Suzanne I. Barchers. Teacher Ideas Press. 1-800-237-6124.

Robber Girl: No you won't, Mother! I have wanted someone to play with, and she will do nicely. She can give me her pretty clothes and take care of me. Tell me, girl, are you a princess?

Gerda: No, I am only a poor girl who is searching for my friend Kay. I fear he was kidnapped, and I haven't been able to find him.

Robber Queen: She is useless to us, and I think we should just kill her now.

Robber Girl: No, Mother, you are not to kill her, but if she misbehaves I will kill her myself!

Second Narrator: They all went to the robbers' camp, where Gerda slept. Later, she was awakened by the cooing of a wood pigeon.

Wood Pigeon: Gerda, we have seen your friend Kay. He was sitting in the Snow Queen's sleigh, which drove through the forest.

Gerda: Where did she go?

Wood Pigeon: The Snow Queen loves the ice and snow and probably went to Lapland, where it is always wintery. But the reindeer knows more than we do about Lapland and can probably help you find the way.

First Narrator: Gerda went to the reindeer, who told her that he indeed knew the way to the Snow Queen. Once it turned dark, Gerda climbed on the reindeer, and they flew over the ground as fast as the reindeer could go. Finally, they came to Lapland and stopped at the house of an old woman. Gerda told the old woman how she was searching for Kay and asked for her help.

Lapland Woman: You have much farther to go, you poor creatures. You must go more than a hundred miles into Finland, for that is where the Snow Queen lives.

Gerda: How do we get there?

Lapland Woman: I will write the directions for you on this dried fish, for I have no paper. Give it to the Finland woman, for she can give you better advice than I can.

Second Narrator: Gerda warmed herself and ate while the Lapland woman wrote out the directions. Then she and the reindeer dashed off for Finland. They found the way easily because the night was bright with the Northern Lights. Soon they knocked at the Finland woman's home, and Gerda shared her story, asking for the Finland woman's help.

Finland Woman: Little Kay is with the Snow Queen, but I am afraid he likes it there very well. You see, he has a splinter of glass in his heart and a bit in his eye. Until these come out he will never be free, and the Snow Queen will keep her power over him.

Gerda: Can't you give me something that will help me gain his freedom?

Finland Woman: You have so much power already, my dear. Even the birds and beasts help you in your quest for your friend. If you can't conquer the Snow Queen by yourself, there is nothing I can do to help you. Her garden begins two miles from here, but the reindeer can carry you only as far as the large bush with the red berries.

First Narrator: Gerda and the reindeer set off again, but in their haste Gerda forgot her gloves and boots. She felt the bitter cold, but could not risk taking the time to return for them. Soon she was standing all alone in the snows of Finland. She began searching again.

Second Narrator: Meanwhile, Kay was quite content inside a palace of driven snow with doors and windows of piercing wind. All the halls, made of frozen snow, were lit by the Northern Lights, and they glittered with ice. The great hall, where the Snow Queen enjoyed sitting, was a frozen lake that had cracked into a thousand pieces. Kay didn't feel the cold, thanks to the Snow Queen's freezing kisses and the sliver of glass in his heart. He played with the pieces of ice, trying to make them into the word "love," because the Snow Queen had told him that if he could spell out the word she would give him his freedom and a new pair of skates.

Kay: I can't spell it properly, no matter how hard I try.

Snow Queen: Well, Kay, you just stay here and play. I am off to warmer countries to bring them a dusting of snow.

First Narrator: She flew off, leaving Kay alone, trying to solve his puzzle. He sat so still that he appeared to be frozen, and this is exactly when Gerda entered the hall.

Gerda: Oh, Kay, I have found you at last!

Second Narrator: But Kay sat so still and cold that Gerda began to hug him and cry great hot tears. As she cried, her tears warmed his heart, sweeping away the piece of the looking glass. He looked at her and burst into tears, washing out the splinter in his eye so that he could finally recognize his dear friend.

Kay: Gerda, where have you been? And where have I been? What is this cold place, anyway?

First Narrator: Gerda kissed Kay's hands and together they spelled out the word "love" in the sparkling ice. They talked about Grandmother, Gerda's journey and adventures, and going home. Finally, they hurried back to the bush where they found the reindeer waiting for them. The reindeer took them to the Finland woman, who fed them and gave them advice for their journey home.

From *Multicultural Folktales: Readers Theatre for Elementary Students.* © 2000 Suzanne I. Barchers. Teacher Ideas Press. 1-800-237-6124.

Second Narrator: Then they went to the Lapland woman, who gave them new clothes and a sleigh. The reindeer took them to the forest, where the fields were green and fresh. Soon they saw home and found Grandmother waiting for them. Everything was just as it had been, but when they went through the doorway they found they had both grown up into young adults.

First Narrator: And best of all, it was summer, warm glorious summer.

from Teacher Ideas Press

FIFTY FABULOUS FABLES: Beginning Readers Theatre
Suzanne I. Barchers

Suzanne Barchers has done it again. Engross young children in reading and learning with these charming readers theatre scripts based on traditional fables from around the world. Each has been evaluated with the Flesch-Kincaid Readability Scale and includes tips for presentation, props, and delivery. **Grades 1–4.**
x, 137p. 8½x11 paper ISBN 1-56308-553-4

SCARY READERS THEATRE
Suzanne I. Barchers

Deliciously ghostly, startling, and downright scary scripts will make you and your students listen, ponder, shiver, chuckle, or even jump! Based on 30 folktales, myths, ghost stories, and legends, these reproducible scripts have been evaluated using the Flesch-Kincaid Readability Scale. **Grades 2–5.**
xiii, 157p. 8½x11 paper ISBN 1-56308-292-6

TADPOLE TALES AND OTHER TOTALLY TERRIFIC TREATS FOR READERS THEATRE
Anthony D. Fredericks

These wild and wacky adaptations of Mother Goose rhymes and traditional fairy tales will fill your classroom with laughter and learning! Featuring more than 25 reproducible scripts, an assortment of unfinished plays and titles, and practical guidelines for using readers theatre in the classroom, this book is a perfect resource for primary educators. **Grades 1–4.**
xii, 139p. 8½x11 paper ISBN 1-56308-547-X

Also by Suzanne Barchers:

• **COOKING UP U.S. HISTORY**
  Recipes and Research to Share with Children, 2d Edition
  Suzanne I. Barchers and Patricia C. Marden
  Grades 1–6. *ISBN 1-56308-682-4*

• **BRIDGES TO READING, K–3 AND 3–6**
  Teaching Reading Skills with Children's Literature
  Suzanne I. Barchers
  Grades K–3: ISBN 1-56308-758-8
  Grades 3–6: ISBN 1-56308-759-6

For a free catalog or to place an order, please contact: Teacher Ideas Press/Libraries Unlimited at 1-800-237-6124 or
• **Fax: 303-220-8843**
• **E-mail: lu-books@lu.com**
• **Mail to: Dept. B002 • P.O. Box 6633**
  Englewood, CO 80155-6633